Understanding Academic Freedom

Understanding Academic Freedom

Henry Reichman

Johns Hopkins University Press · *Baltimore*

Johns Hopkins University Press
2715 North Charles Street
Baltimore, Maryland 21218-4363
www.press.jhu.edu

Library of Congress Cataloging-in-Publication Data

Names: Reichman, Henry, 1947– author.
Title: Understanding academic freedom / Henry Reichman.
Description: Baltimore, Maryland : Johns Hopkins University Press, 2021. |
    Series: Higher ed leadership essentials | Includes bibliographical
    references and index.
Identifiers: LCCN 2020056262 | ISBN 9781421442150 (paperback) |
    ISBN 9781421442167 (ebook)
Subjects: LCSH: Academic freedom—United States. | Education, Higher—Political
    aspects—United States. | Education and state—United States.
Classification: LCC LC72.2 .R453 2021 | DDC 378.1/21—dc23
LC record available at https://lccn.loc.gov/2020056262

A catalog record for this book is available from the British Library.

*Special discounts are available for bulk purchases of this book. For more information,
please contact Special Sales at specialsales@jh.edu.*

To
All college and university faculty members unjustly dismissed
in violation of their academic freedom
and
All who have suffered or died because their "leaders"
denied science

Contents

Understanding Academic Freedom

Introduction

A community college instructor in Iowa is pressured to resign after his pro-antifa social media comments garner threats and vicious harassment that administrators find threatening to campus safety. A tenured biology professor at a college on Long Island is threatened with dismissal because she is alleged to grade students too strictly. A tenured law professor in California is dismissed despite a unanimous ruling in her favor by a university-wide faculty committee, purportedly for making threatening comments but in reality for being a campus gadfly. Another law professor in Georgia is spared dismissal for language used in class only after a faculty committee rejects efforts to fire him. In New York City a long-serving adjunct writing instructor loses a nearly three-year effort to keep her position when an arbitrator rules against her on the basis of just two negative comments in student evaluations. In Washington state another adjunct instructor is dismissed after decades of teaching for a minor violation of rules: she had been a leader in an unsuccessful effort to win a union contract. In Washington, DC, a private university fires a conservative professor for tweets about prominent Democratic politicians that it deems "inconsistent with the respect for human dignity." In the wake of the COVID-19 pandemic, a conservative activist calls on his followers to take advantage of online classes to send "any and all videos of blatant indoctrination" to his organization so that it might expose and blacklist "leftist professors." The president of a small college in upstate New York uses the pandemic as an opportunity to "eliminate tenure" and "re-work the grievance process" to prohibit its application to "hiring/firing issues." At a private university in San Diego, the administration responds to the pandemic by unilaterally voiding faculty contracts, revamping curriculum without faculty participation, and announcing that in future instructors will no longer be entitled to "individual academic freedom in the classroom."[1]

These incidents all date from the 2019/20 academic year and represent only the tip of a larger iceberg. Academic freedom, long heralded as a core value of American higher education, may now be in as much danger as at any time since the dark days of the 1950s anti-Communist hysteria. And if academic freedom is threatened, so too is education itself. As the philosopher and educator John Dewey wrote in 1902: "Any attack, or even any restriction, upon academic freedom is directed against the university itself. To investigate truth; critically to verify fact; to reach conclusions by means of the best methods at command, untrammeled by external fear or favor, to communicate this truth to the student; to interpret to him its bearing on the questions he will have to face in life—this is precisely the aim and object of the university. To aim a blow at any one of these operations is to deal a vital wound to the university itself." Moreover, Dewey added, "Since freedom of mind and freedom of expression are the root of all freedom, to deny freedom in education is a crime against democracy."[2]

But what is meant when we use the term *academic freedom*? For many, these words have become little more than a shibboleth, piously intoned by professors, administrators, and trustees alike—even by politicians—but far too often rendered meaningless by the action or, many times, the inaction of those who invoke them. For some the term has degenerated into a call for individual academic license, the alleged right of faculty members to teach whatever and however they wish or to say whatever comes to mind, regardless of scholarly validity. For others, it is a value to be upheld for supporters, but not for opponents in some polarizing controversy. For still others, academic freedom has degenerated into a narrow claim of privilege by a professorial elite, insulated from public accountability, even as, for the great majority who teach—on term contracts and mostly part-time—such freedom seems unattainable.

This book mounts a defense of academic freedom by probing its role in multiple contexts, thereby offering readers an introduction to and exploration of the concept. It strives to elucidate the term's sometimes complicated meanings and uses for faculty members, administrators, trustees, journalists, politicians, and anyone with an interest in higher education's future. Like its close cousin, freedom of speech, academic freedom cannot easily be defined by a set of ironclad rules or enumerated in a standard list of dos and don'ts. It emerges out of the contextual application of guiding principles, developed and modified over time. It is an aspirational value, like equality or liberty, defined best in its usage. As Louis Menand has argued, it would be misleading to assume that "there exists some unproblematic conception of academic freedom that is philosophically coherent and that will conduce to outcomes in particular cases which all parties will feel to be just and equitable."[3] Hence, this book is not a manual for the application of rigid dogma. It devotes space to describing difficult situations in which people of good faith may differ, and there may be no obviously "correct" way to apply accepted values.

If there is fluidity to what academic freedom may mean in practice, however, its theoretical definition still establishes clear parameters. The book takes as its starting point a basic understanding that academic freedom, as developed and practiced in the United States, is not a civil right, as is freedom of speech, nor is it simply an individual employment benefit provided to those in a restricted number of academic appointments. It is, instead, a freedom belonging to the academic profession as a whole to pursue inquiry and teach freely, limited and guided by the principles of that profession. Academic freedom guarantees to both faculty members and students the right to engage in intellectual inquiry and debate without fear of censorship or retaliation. It grants considerable scope to the consciences of individual teachers and researchers, but it functions ultimately as the collective freedom of the scholarly community to govern itself in the interest of serving the common good in a democratic society. As the AAUP's 1956 response to the excesses of the McCarthy era put it, "The demand we of the academic world make for academic freedom is not made primarily for our own benefit. We enjoy the exercise of freedom; but the purposes of liberty lie, in a democracy, in the common welfare."[4]

Following a brief survey of the history of academic freedom's development in the United States, three chapters address the concept's main components: freedom in research and the publication of research results; freedom in teaching; and freedom from institutional discipline for public statements made by professors as citizens and as stewards of their institutions, including on topics removed from their academic expertise. This is followed by discussions of the much maligned and misunderstood institution of tenure and the rise of contingent faculty employment, the gravest current threat to academic freedom; the development, since the 1950s, of an academic freedom jurisprudence based on the US Constitution, applicable principally to public institutions and differing in key respects from the professional understanding of the term upheld in this book; and the rights of students in and out of class, including treatment of student protest movements. In these chapters much space is devoted to detailing specific cases. This reflects academic freedom's development through concrete experience and contested argument.

The final chapter returns to academic freedom's foundational rationale to argue that its protection and revitalization are critical if our democracy is to reverse the deleterious effects of anti-intellectual assaults on expertise, knowledge, and, ultimately, truth itself. A brief appendix recapitulates the major principles emerging from the preceding narrative.

Because academic freedom in the United States has been most persistently and vigorously defended as a professional standard by the American Association of University Professors (AAUP), that organization's definition and development of the concept constitutes the book's central thread, although at times other approaches are considered, especially in the treatment of the judiciary's halting and contradictory creation of a First Amendment doctrine of academic freedom.

Chapter 1

History

The roots of academic freedom can be traced to universities in medieval Europe, but the ideal came to the United States in the last decades of the nineteenth century from Germany. At that time American higher education was rapidly transforming from a system of small, regional, and largely denominational colleges offering a mostly classical curriculum for the education and moral upbringing of middle-class and wealthy elites into one dominated by rapidly expanding secular research institutions offering undergraduate, advanced, and professional degrees. After the Civil War, Americans seeking an academic career in this changing environment often went for their training to Germany, which boasted the most sophisticated university system in Europe. There they encountered and were much impressed by the ideal of *Akademische Freiheit*.

In 1811, the philosopher Johann Gottlieb Fichte, serving as rector of the University of Jena, proclaimed the "free investigation of every object of thought" to be a human right essential to the pursuit of *Wissenschaft*, most often translated as "science" but indicating more broadly all manner of systematic and disciplined inquiry. For German scholars, academic freedom encompassed both *Lernfreiheit*, the freedom of the student to seek knowledge without restriction, and *Lehrfreiheit*, the freedom of the professor to teach in accordance with the precepts of a scholarly discipline. Although sympathetic to the rights of students, American academics returning from Germany were concerned chiefly with establishing their own rights, their *Lehrfreiheit*, in the emerging research and teaching institutions of Gilded Age America.

In Germany, higher education was centralized and its universities were extensions of the state. Faculties were concerned as much with establishing and defending the autonomy of their institutions against government tutelage as with their individual freedom to teach and conduct research as they pleased. The result was a compromise in which the imperial state guaranteed institutional autonomy and the right of the faculty to self-govern in exchange for political conformity. *Akademische Freiheit* made a clear distinction between the freedom of scholars within the university, which was extensive, and their rights outside it, which to a considerable degree were not. German academics could claim independence as scholars, but as citizens their liberty could be constrained in ways unsuitable for a society proclaiming democratic ideals.

By contrast to Germany, American colleges and universities, both private and public, were controlled not by government or by their faculties but by independent governing boards, as remains the case today. These boards delegated authority not to professors but to frequently autocratic administrations. While earlier boards had been dominated by clergy, by 1900 their composition had shifted. Most trustees were by then businessmen, who often understood their institutions as servants of corporate interests. In this context, the German ideal was transformed and democratized.

Two complementary impulses spurred American scholars to organize. The first was their search for disciplinary and professional authority. The United States in the late nineteenth century witnessed a sweeping movement for professionalization in medicine, law, and other fields, including scholarship. Newly formed scholarly bodies, such as the American Economic Association and the American Political Science Association, sought to establish and defend the privileges of their respective disciplines. At the same time, there was a growing sense that the academic profession as a whole needed to speak as one against the domination of educational institutions by trustees and administrators. Scholarship, it was felt, was itself a vocation that demanded professional autonomy and voice. A literature of professors' protest emerged, collected in 1913 in a thick volume edited by Columbia University psychologist James McKeen Cattell and titled *University Control*. In these writings professors railed against hierarchical management of their institutions by nonscholars and petty tyrants. They demanded to be treated as independent professionals and called for the democratization of university governance. "No one believes that a city should be owned by a small self-perpetuating board of trustees who would appoint a dictator to run it, to decide what people could live there, what work they must do and what incomes they should have," Cattell wrote. "Why should a university be conducted in that way?"[1]

These professors were expressing a broader democratic impulse fueling the progressive agitation of the time. If they were calling for the kind of professional autonomy and intellectual freedom found in Germany, they also understood themselves to be citizens of a democratic society and participants in a broadly progressive movement for expanding democracy in both state and society. Scholarship, they believed, could not ignore the sweeping economic and social changes of the era, nor could it stand aside from reforming efforts to address those changes politically. Professionalism and progressivism could be in tension with each other, then as now, but both were essential to the emerging American version of academic freedom.

The American ideal of academic freedom was influenced too by the national tradition of constitutionally protected free speech, and it is no coincidence that it was during these years that modern First Amendment doctrine also emerged. As we shall see in subsequent chapters, academic freedom and freedom of speech differ in important ways, but in a sense their fates are connected. This can be seen in a series of early conflicts over academic freedom that rallied faculty members and crystallized their concerns.

Even before the German influence was felt, American scientists had won a series of battles against governing boards dominated by churchmen over the right to espouse the Darwinian theory of evolution. Social scientists had also fought for the right to apply those theories to human affairs, although too often in a Social Darwinist manner that today would be deemed racist. These conflicts brought together scholars from various fields who embraced evolutionary theories and sought to defend them against doctrinal moralism, with appeals to the authority of science. In 1878, Alexander Winchell was fired from his position teaching geology at Vanderbilt University by its president, a church bishop, because his support for evolution ran "contrary to the 'plan of redemption.'" The next year, Yale's president attacked William Graham Sumner for his use of evolutionary sociologist Herbert Spencer's writing in an undergraduate course. Historian Walter Metzger has argued that the American rationale for academic freedom would not exist "without the canons of evolutionary science."[2]

By the 1890s, however, the battle had shifted, as businessmen replaced clerics on boards of trustees. In 1894, Richard Ely was attacked for "teaching socialism" at the University of Wisconsin, and Edward Bemis was dismissed after he delivered a speech critical of the railroad companies during the Pullman strike. In 1901, the iconic case of Edward Ross involved that economist's dismissal from Stanford University by Jane Stanford, then the university's sole trustee, in response to his public support for trade unionism.

It is often argued that these cases gave rise to the formation, in January 1915, of the AAUP, but, as Hans-Joerg Tiede has demonstrated, the association's founders were concerned with academic freedom less as an end in itself and more as a means for ensuring professional autonomy and university governance reform. Almost immediately upon the AAUP's formation, however, developments at the University of Utah, where several professors were dismissed arbitrarily "for the good of the institution," and at the University of Pennsylvania, where the socialist Scott Nearing was fired in response to sustained agitation by conservative alumni, compelled the new group to focus almost exclusively on protecting academic freedom. Indeed, in its first year the AAUP investigated five cases in which violations of academic freedom were alleged. The result was the 1915 *Declaration of Principles on Academic Freedom and Academic Tenure*, "the crowning achievement of the AAUP's first year" and the first and arguably most thorough formulation of the American doctrine of academic freedom.[3]

The 1915 Declaration

The 1915 *Declaration* defined academic freedom as comprising "three elements: freedom of inquiry and research; freedom of teaching within the university or college; and freedom of extramural utterance and action." These would remain at the core of future definitions of the concept, although sometimes a fourth freedom—"intramural utterance," speech as a member of the academic community—is extrapolated from the others and justified by the *Declaration*'s lengthy discussions of "the basis of academic authority, the nature of the academic calling, and the function of the academic institution."

The *Declaration* rejected the notion that a university is "an ordinary business venture" and academic teaching "a purely private employment." Instead, it asserted that professors "are the appointees, but not in any proper sense the employees" of the university. "Once appointed, the scholar has professional functions to perform in which the appointing authorities have neither competency nor moral right to intervene. The responsibility of the university teacher is primarily to the public itself and to the judgment of his own profession."

Colleges and universities, public or private, the *Declaration* proclaimed, are "a public trust" devoted to advancing "the sum of human knowledge," providing instruction to students, and developing experts for public service. These functions cannot be fulfilled "without accepting and enforcing to the fullest extent the principle of academic freedom. The responsibility of the university as a whole is to the community at large, and any restriction upon the freedom of the instructor is bound to react injuriously . . . upon the interests of the community." As a public trust, universities must be "so free that no fair-minded person shall find any excuse for even a suspicion that the utterances of university teachers are shaped or restricted by the judgment not of professional scholars, but of inexpert and possibly not wholly disinterested persons outside of their ranks." This is critical because "there is a real danger that pressure from vested interests may, sometimes deliberately and sometimes unconsciously, sometimes openly and sometimes subtly and in obscure ways, be brought to bear upon academic authorities." Here the search for professional autonomy merged with the progressive sympathies of the *Declaration*'s authors. "No person of intelligence believes that all of our political problems have been solved," they wrote. "Grave issues in the adjustment of men's social and economic relations are certain to call for settlement in years that are to come. . . . Toward this settlement the university has potentially its own very great contribution to make."

But if institutions of higher education are a public trust in service of democracy and reform, the *Declaration*'s authors also acknowledged "the dangers connected with the existence in a democracy of an overwhelming and concentrated public opinion." Hence colleges and universities must provide "an inviolable refuge from such tyranny." The university, they declared, should be an intellectual experiment station, where new ideas may germinate and their fruit, though still distasteful to the community as a whole, may be allowed to ripen until finally, perchance, it may become a part of the accepted intellectual food of the nation or of the world. Not less is it a distinctive duty of the university to be the conservator of all genuine elements of value in the past thought and life of mankind which are not in the fashion of the moment. . . . The university is, indeed, likely always to exercise a certain form of conservative influence. . . . One of its most characteristic functions in a democratic society is to help make public opinion more self-critical and more circumspect, to check the more hasty and unconsidered impulses of popular feeling, to train the democracy to the habit of looking before and after. It is precisely this function of the university which is most injured by any restriction upon academic freedom.

Universities exist to serve the public, the *Declaration* asserted, but to do so they must guarantee the professional autonomy of their faculties and protect their professional judgment. "Only those who carry on their work in the temper of the scientific inquirer" may assert claims to academic freedom. "The liberty of the scholar within the university to set forth his conclusions . . . is conditioned by their being conclusions gained by a scholar's method and held in a scholar's spirit." Hence the *Declaration* insisted that disciplinary and professional standards "cannot with safety" be enforced "by bodies not composed of the academic profession." To ensure such enforcement, the *Declaration* called for the creation of "suitable judicial bodies, composed of members of the academic profession, which may be called into action before university teachers are dismissed or disciplined, and may determine in what cases the question of academic freedom is actually involved."

It is essential to recognize that academic freedom was not here conceived as an individual right of professors to do whatever they wish in their research and teaching or to say whatever they might in public remarks. To be sure, it is difficult if not impossible to imagine academic freedom being secure without assurances that individual scholars can be protected, including, as we shall see in chapter 4, in their often controversial, even inflammatory, comments as citizens on topics sometimes well removed from their disciplinary expertise. Nevertheless, the *Declaration* proudly asserted that it was "not the absolute freedom of utterance of the individual scholar, but the absolute freedom of thought, of inquiry, of discussion and of teaching, of the academic profession that is asserted by this declaration of principles." Academic freedom, in short, commits the professoriate not only to freedom in teaching and research but also to compliance with disciplinary and professional standards. Notwithstanding legitimate fears that an established faculty can abuse its power to enforce those standards, absent such a commitment to professionalism, Matthew Finkin and Robert Post assert, public support for academic freedom would vanish.[4]

The AAUP justified both professional autonomy and academic freedom by their contributions to the "common good." The conservative writer Russell Kirk would decades later offer another more individualist justification. It will be worth a brief digression to look at his approach. Kirk's 1955 book *Academic Freedom: An Essay in Definition* was written partly in response to William F. Buckley Jr.'s *God and Man at Yale,* arguably the founding text of American conservatism's hostility to the academy. Although he believed that scholarship was ultimately of benefit to the common good, Kirk did not justify academic freedom by its societal impact. He called the scholar "the guardian of the word," arguing that academic freedom is founded on "the enduring idea of a special liberty, or body of liberties, that is attached to the academic institution, the teacher, and the scholar." Instead of conceiving the university as a public trust, Kirk argued that "the principal importance of academic freedom is the opportunity it affords for the highest development of private reason and imagination, the improvement of mind and heart by the apprehension of Truth, whether or not that development is of any immediate use to [society]. . . . The theory of academic freedom is that the search after Truth involves certain risks: for Truth is not always popular in the marketplace, and there are opinions and fields of speculation that cannot prudently be discussed in the daily press or in the public meetings."

In a hostile review Buckley wrote that Kirk "blandly assumes that all teachers are scholars," when most are in fact "sophists." But Kirk explicitly recognized the presence of such alleged sophists. His opposition to Buckley's approach arose from fear that if the sophists were rooted out, a great many philosophers would be rooted out with them. "It is only out of concern for the Philosophers that the Sophists are tolerated in their license," he wrote. Indeed, "it is part of the duty of the philosopher to preserve freedom in the Academy even for the sophist." Kirk's ivory-towerish justification for academic freedom differed from that of the AAUP's founders, rooted as they were in both the progressivism and engaged professionalism of their era. Programmatically, however, Kirk's approach could join in common cause with the AAUP, and it is worth noting how sharply his views differ from those embraced today by most conservative politicians.[5]

In its initial three years the AAUP investigated thirty-five alleged violations of academic freedom. This experience established the practice, continuing today, of producing detailed reports on critical incidents—supplemented since the 1930s by establishment of a standing list of institutions whose administrations have been censured for violations of academic freedom on the basis of these investigations—which collectively can be seen as a rich body of extralegal case law and a source for the development of subsequent policy statements. The purpose of the AAUP's investigations has been "to warn and to illustrate, rather than to avenge and redress."[6] While not always carried out with efficiency, they have by and large had a salutary impact on the atmosphere for academic freedom, despite having only the power of moral suasion. Taken as a whole, the association's investigation reports comprise a body of "academic common law" that has at times been recognized as a source of authority in the nation's courts.

Individual cases do not always reveal the extent to which more systematic efforts to impose orthodoxy can quiet dissenting voices, however. The entry of the United States into World War I offers an early illustration. If previously religious faith and business interests were perceived as potential threats, it would now become clear that nationalism and patriotism could also imperil academic freedom. As the professoriate, like the country as a whole, was gripped by a wartime cult of loyalty, instructors lost their jobs. One historian has counted some twenty known cases of dismissal or non-reappointment, but this was likely the tip of the iceberg. Sadly, most of the AAUP's leaders embraced the patriotism of the day, several even producing anti-German propaganda, and the association not only failed to defend professors who were dismissed but also endorsed wartime restrictions on expression extending even to speech "not expressly forbidden by law."

The 1940 Statement

The aftermath of the war would see an upsurge of unrest among college and university faculty members. Some would embrace unionization, but that movement was, for the time being, short-lived, and the AAUP would turn instead to efforts to codify and win broader support from the higher education community for the principles of the 1915 *Declaration.* In 1925, the American Council on Education convened a meeting of organizations, including the AAUP, that produced a joint statement on academic freedom. The statement was weak, however, and failed to win significant approval from faculties or administrations. A decade later the AAUP gained support for a new effort from the Association of American Colleges (AAC; now the Association of American Colleges and Universities), which represented administrations at many liberal arts and denominational colleges. In 1936, the two groups entered negotiations for a successor statement to the 1915 *Declaration.* An agreement reflecting concessions by each party was reached two years later, but the AAC balked at signing, which compelled further compromise before the two groups issued the 1940 *Statement of Principles on Academic Freedom and Tenure.*[7]

The 1940 *Statement* has since become the standard definition of academic freedom in the United States, consistent in principle with the lengthier 1915 document and now associated more with the AAUP than with its administrative partner. It has been endorsed by more than 250 academic associations and disciplinary societies, its provisions included in countless faculty handbooks and collective bargaining agreements. A 2020 study found that "almost three-quarters of institutions with a tenure system (73 percent) base their academic freedom policy directly on the 1940 *Statement,*" and "more than half cite the AAUP as the source of their policy."[8]

Following the lead of the AAUP's founders, the 1940 *Statement* declared that "institutions of higher education are conducted for the common good and not to further the interest of either the individual teacher or the institution as a whole. The common good depends upon the free search for truth and its free exposition. Academic freedom is essential to these purposes and applies to both teaching and research." This "common good" justification, while consistent with the approach of the 1915 *Declaration,* nonetheless placed somewhat reduced emphasis on professional autonomy.

The *Statement*'s definition of academic freedom's three components is worth quoting in full:

1. Teachers are entitled to full freedom in research and in the publication of the results, subject to the adequate performance of their other academic duties; but research for pecuniary return should be based upon an understanding with the authorities of the institution.

2. Teachers are entitled to freedom in the classroom in discussing their subject, but they should be careful not to introduce into their teaching controversial matter which has no relation to their subject. Limitations of academic freedom because of religious or other aims of the institution should be clearly stated in writing at the time of the appointment.

3. College and university teachers are citizens, members of a learned profession, and officers of an educational institution. When they speak or write as citizens, they should be free from institutional censorship or discipline, but their special position in the community imposes special obligations. As scholars and educational officers, they should remember that the public may judge their profession and their institution by their utterances. Hence they should at all times be accurate, should exercise appropriate restraint, should show respect for the opinions of others, and should make every effort to indicate that they are not speaking for the institution.

Each of these principles will be explored in subsequent chapters, but suffice it for now to say that the *Statement* demands repeated interpretation and application to concrete situations. In 1947, the AAUP's Committee A on Academic Freedom and Tenure observed how its "full meaning, like the meaning of provisions of the Constitution of the United States, is subject to gradual discovery . . . as the principles are applied to case after case."

For the AAUP the *Statement* represented an endorsement by an administrative partner of the ideal of tenure proposed in 1915 and further concretized the terms that would make tenure effective. This marked a significant advance. Tenure, the 1940 *Statement* declared, "is a means to certain ends," those being both protection of the academic freedoms defined by the *Statement* and assurance of "a sufficient degree of economic security to make the profession attractive to men and women of ability." In 1915, the AAUP's founders had called for tenure after ten years of service, but the 1940 document declared that "the probationary period should not exceed seven years."

The Post–World War II Era

The massive expansion of American higher education after World War II, initiated by the GI Bill and fueled by economic growth and the demands of the Cold War, saw increasingly widespread adoption of the principles articulated in the 1940 *Statement*, despite the AAUP's own failure to mount an effective national response to the anti-Communist hysteria of the early 1950s until after much of the damage had been done. Those years, characterized by loyalty oaths and dismissals of professors who declined to testify before witch-hunting congressional bodies, were dark ones for academic freedom, but they would in the end produce for the first time a legal, First Amendment-based conception of academic freedom, applicable mainly to public institutions and highly ambiguous (see chapter 6). The Red Scare notwithstanding, the two postwar decades saw demand for college and university teachers expand dramatically, compelling institutions that had previously declined to adopt tenure systems to do so if they wished to attract qualified instructors and researchers. By the 1970s, some two-thirds of those teaching in American higher education were either tenured or probationary for tenure, and the 1940 principles were widely endorsed, if far from consistently adhered to in practice.

In the American South, the Red Scare of the '50s merged with a "black scare" arising out of opposition to desegregation, fueling white southern hostility to academic freedom in higher education and prompting action by the AAUP, as Joy Ann Williamson-Lott has shown. "Between 1955 and 1965 the association became heavily involved in southern higher education by censuring institutions that fired professors who espoused support for racial equality, issuing resolutions, and publishing reports on the southern situation."[9] In 1965, an extraordinary report on the state of academic freedom in Mississippi examined several outstanding individual cases but also commented extensively on the condition of higher education in the state based on first-hand investigation by a special committee. The report found "no improper limitation or restriction placed on an instructor's right to express his views in classroom lectures and discussions," even if many faculty members "exercised a certain amount of self-restraint." Freedom of extramural expression was another matter. The committee found "an almost total unanimity among faculty members, administrators, and state officials" that such expression was "severely hampered," as a matter "primarily of fear." The report concluded that in an "atmosphere of intensely conflicting feelings, arising out of the encounter between a rapidly changing social situation and an almost pathological xenophobia concerning ideas which are believed to be subversive of the traditional way of life, conditions of academic freedom are precarious."[10]

Higher education has not been exempt from the country's ongoing failure to fully grapple with systemic racism and the legacy of racial slavery. For that reason it may be understandable if some see protection of academic freedom as merely an aspect of the protection of largely white, elite privilege. That claim will be addressed at several points in chapters to come, but for now it will be useful to note how the country's foremost advocate for academic freedom historically viewed the relation between academic freedom and inequality.

In 1973, the AAUP published a report, *Affirmative Action in Higher Education*, which started from "the premise that discrimination against women and minorities in higher education is both reprehensible and illegal, and reaffirm[ed] the emphatic condemnation of such practices by the AAUP." The report found affirmative action to mean "essentially the revision of standards and practices to assure that institutions are in fact drawing from the largest marketplace of human resources in staffing their faculties, and a critical review of appointment and advancement criteria to insure that they do not inadvertently foreclose consideration of the best qualified persons by untested presuppositions which operate to exclude women and minorities." It added that "the politics of reaction are a greater source for concern than the possibility that affirmative action might lend itself to heavy-handed bureaucratic misapplication." In a reflective conclusion, which from the vantage point of today reads like a warning not yet fully heeded, the report predicted that affirmative action would be a test revealing whether professors are "what we say we are; that we mean to be fair, that our concern with excellence is not a subterfuge, that we are concerned to be just in the civil rights of all persons in the conduct of our profession." The authors continued, "We do not doubt in this respect that institutions of higher learning will thus reveal more about themselves in the manner in which they respond to the call for affirmative action, however, than what their response may reveal about the consistency of such plans with excellence and fairness in higher education."[11]

Lernfreiheit and Governance

Partly in response to student activism in the civil rights movement and to the Berkeley Free Speech Movement (FSM), in 1967 the AAUP, the AAC, and several other administrative and student groups issued the *Joint Statement on the Rights and Freedoms of Students*, the most extensive explication of *Lernfreiheit* in American higher education (discussed in chapter 7).[12] It declared that "freedom to teach and freedom to learn are inseparable facets of academic freedom," adding that "all members of the academic community" are "responsible for safeguarding the freedom to learn."

Although after 1915 the AAUP's focus had shifted to protecting academic freedom, the organization did not abandon its initial concerns with reforming structures of university governance and protecting faculty rights within those structures. A landmark 1933 AAUP investigation into the dismissal of faculty members at Rollins College, a progressive institution in Florida, found that, while protecting controversial professors' social and political views was not an issue, the refusal of the college president and its trustees to abandon "the long-established practice of sole and complete authority over all college matters" and accept the faculty's jurisdiction over academic policy was.[13] In 1938, an AAUP committee concluded that "a university or a college is in essence a group of scholars cooperating in an educational task, and conducting that task essentially by discussion and mutual conviction. The future of university education . . . depends upon our ability to find the kind of institutions in which our conception can be embodied and to give to the government of universities a form such that cooperative scholarship may find therein its organs."

By the mid-1960s the association was able to engage first the American Council on Education and then the Association of Governing Boards of Universities and Colleges to produce the joint *Statement on Government of Colleges and Universities*.[14] Defining the functions respectively of governing board, administration, and faculty, and calling for "appropriate joint planning and effort" among the three, this 1966 *Statement* delineated the responsibilities of the faculty in such a way as to support academic freedom and justify the faculty's authority:

> The faculty has primary responsibility for such fundamental areas as curriculum, subject matter and methods of instruction, research, faculty status, and those aspects of student life which relate to the educational process. On these matters the power of review or final decision lodged in the governing board or delegated by it to the president should be exercised adversely only in exceptional circumstances, and for reasons communicated to the faculty. . . .
>
> Faculty status and related matters are primarily a faculty responsibility; this area includes appointments, reappointments, decisions not to reappoint, promotions, the granting of tenure,

and dismissal. The primary responsibility of the faculty for such matters is based upon the fact that its judgment is central to general educational policy. Furthermore, scholars in a particular field or activity have the chief competence for judging the work of their colleagues; in such competence it is implicit that responsibility exists for both adverse and favorable judgments. . . . The governing board and president should, on questions of faculty status, as in other matters where the faculty has primary responsibility, concur with the faculty judgment except in rare instances and for compelling reasons which should be stated in detail.

To this day the *Statement on Government* remains the standard model for proper university governance, recommended not only by the AAUP but by administrative and trustee organizations as well.

The 1970 Interpretive Comments and After

In 1969, a joint committee of the AAUP and AAC met to reevaluate the 1940 *Statement* in an effort to apply lessons learned over the previous thirty years. Rather than rewriting the statement, the committee created a series of "interpretive comments," now attached to the document as footnotes. These were adopted by the AAUP in 1970. Perhaps the most consequential comment addressed the *Statement*'s seemingly uncertain stance on the protection of faculty expression "as citizens," and will be discussed in chapter 4.

The 1970 interpretive comments also lent greater clarity to the 1940 *Statement*'s guarantees of due process protections for tenured and probationary faculty subject to discipline or dismissal. These have been developed further in a series of policy statements on such matters as procedural standards in dismissal proceedings and renewal and nonrenewal of appointments, on standards for non-reappointment, access to personnel files, and the "use and abuse" of faculty suspensions. In addition, the

AAUP continually updates and revises its *Recommended Institutional Regulations on Academic Freedom and Tenure,* first formulated in 1957 and adopted in their current basic form in 1968, with further modifications over the years since, most recently in 2018.[15] These regulations seek to present, in language appropriate for use in college and university policy documents, rules that derive from the chief provisions and interpretations of the 1940 *Statement.*

In the 1960s, efforts to unionize college and university faculties revived and gained significant traction. By the early 1970s the AAUP had itself embraced unionism. Fears that a commitment to collective bargaining might undermine the association's traditional dedication to academic freedom have proven unwarranted, however. As a recent comprehensive study demonstrates, "collective bargaining can complicate but has not endangered" the AAUP's academic freedom work.[16] While the largest portion of current AAUP members are in chapters with collective bargaining agreements, most unionized faculty are members of other unions. Many of these have also come to adopt AAUP standards on academic freedom, and collective bargaining agreements often reference them.

Over the past several decades the AAUP has, in addition to its investigative reports, produced a series of policy statements designed to further define the meaning of academic freedom. These include statements on academic freedom and tenure in medical schools, on academic freedom in the arts, on electronic communications and social media, and on politically controversial academic personnel decisions, all collected in *AAUP Policy Documents and Reports,* known more commonly as the Red Book, now in its eleventh edition. In 1972, the AAUP, the AAC, and the Association of College and Research Libraries, a division of the American Library Association, produced the *Joint Statement on Faculty Status of College and Research Librarians,* which declared that "academic freedom is indispensable to librarians in their roles as teachers and researchers. Critically, they are trustees of knowledge with the responsibility of ensuring the intellectual freedom of the academic community through the availability of information and ideas, no matter how controversial, so that teachers may freely teach and students may freely learn."[17]

The Erosion of Tenure

Since the 1970s, the proportion of faculty appointments in higher education eligible for tenure has steadily declined to the point that today only about a fourth of those who teach in colleges and universities, including graduate student instructors, are covered by the tenure system. The majority are now hired on contingent contracts for limited term appointments, often on a part-time basis. This baleful development has been a growing concern among faculty of all ranks and has been addressed by the AAUP in a series of policy documents. The unchecked expansion of contingent employment—what has been labeled "the gig academy"—threatens not only the economic security of the profession, which both the 1915 *Declaration* and the 1940 *Statement* recognized as a purpose of continuous tenure, but also academic freedom. In recent years, more and more academic freedom cases have involved faculty members off the tenure track. In several cases the faculty member has been dismissed mid-contract, but far more dangerous is that, under a system of short-term appointments, institutions may quietly decline to renew a contract without public rationale. Thus, for each of these cases there are likely dozens more where faculty members think twice and decide that not speaking is the better part of valor. As one of the AAUP's first investigations—into the dismissal of Scott Nearing— concluded, "It makes little practical difference, so far as the inquiry to academic freedom is concerned," whether a teacher's removal "is called 'non-reappointment,' or 'removal,' or 'dismissal.'" The increasing vulnerability of those outside the tenure system inevitably bleeds into that system itself, potentially rendering the entire professoriate "fearful, insular, and conformist."[18]

As the 2018 revision to the AAUP's *Recommended Institutional Regulations* declared, "There should be no invidious distinctions between those who teach and/or conduct research in higher education, regardless of whether they hold full-time or part-time appointments or whether their appointments are tenured, tenure-track, or contingent. All faculty members should have access to the same due-process protections and procedures."[19] (For a more extensive discussion of tenure and its erosion, see chapter 5.)

Since the 1915 *Declaration* academic freedom has come to be widely embraced as a core principle of higher education in the United States. Even as the tenure system, designed as its strongest defense, erodes, the ideal remains almost universally espoused, even by its enemies. But to a great degree academic freedom has been a victim of its own success, treated too often as a platitude. To be sure, it has always been as much aspiration as reality. Still, as conceived by the authors of the *Declaration*, academic freedom is a kind of public trust, in which scholars and teachers are granted freedom to regulate their work because that work is essential to advancing the common good and informing democratic decision-making, to which the faculty in turn must be dedicated. As such, its defense and advancement are indispensable in a democratic society.

Chapter 2

Research

Both the 1915 *Declaration* and the 1940 *Statement* ranked "freedom of inquiry and research" first among the three components of academic freedom. Yet the 1915 document hastened to acknowledge that this freedom was "almost everywhere so safeguarded that the dangers of its infringement are slight." Certainly, cases involving discipline or dismissal of individual faculty members for the content of their research have been infrequent over the years when compared to cases involving teaching or extramural expression. However, especially if the 1940 inclusion of a right to freedom in the "publication of the results" of research is taken into account, subsequent history suggests that the *Declaration*'s authors were overly sanguine. It may be the case that universities rarely seek to suppress research or discipline faculty members for the content of their scholarly publications. Nevertheless, threats to academic freedom in research can be subtle and systemic in ways not always revealed by notorious cases.

Among the freedoms delineated in the 1940 *Statement,* only freedom of research and publication is described as "full." This would suggest that unlike the instructor's freedom in the classroom, limited by the obligation to discuss the assigned subject and avoid indoctrination, freedom in research should be completely unfettered. In search of new knowledge, scholars must be free to wander wherever their minds may take them, to experiment, to speculate, and to imagine. Moreover, they must be free to share the fruits of their wanderings with colleagues and ultimately the general public in ways and at times of their choosing. On the other hand, their investigations must be guided by "a scholar's method" and presented in "a scholar's spirit." The research protected by academic freedom is not that of dabblers or dilettantes. Researchers must conform to accepted intellectual and disciplinary standards conceived and developed to distinguish scholarship from fraud, originality from eccentricity. Scholars have earned the right to free inquiry precisely because they have been trained in inquiry's *Wissenschaftlich* methods and have by and large accepted its conventions.

Yet standards are developed and defended through consensus, and consensus can stifle genuine innovation and creativity. If intellectual standards are required to justify academic freedom and connect it to the production of new knowledge, those standards "are also themselves forms of knowledge whose evaluation requires academic freedom."[1] Moreover, controversies over the definition, legitimacy, and appropriate application of research methodologies—even of disciplines themselves—abound throughout the academy. At times and in many fields such controversies rest at the very center of heated scholarly debates and may lead to important breakthroughs in knowledge. Nonetheless, if the "full freedom" in research promised by the 1940 *Statement* is to withstand critique, it cannot countenance willful or careless violations of intellectual standards and professional norms. Ultimately, colleges and universities and their faculties assess research efforts and render judgments about those efforts by applying these standards and norms, even if the standards and norms are themselves subject to continual question and correction. In this way practices that may initially impede recognition of fresh approaches may ultimately protect those approaches, once they win greater acceptance.

Nowhere in higher education today is freedom of inquiry and research totally unrestrained. Restrictions by law and peer review are both common and necessary. Judgments must be and are made on a daily basis in hiring, promotion, as well as funding and publishing decisions. This leads to two fundamental questions: What kinds of collegial and institutional restraint are appropriate and which are not? And who is best positioned to define and impose such restraints?

Taking the second question first, it is clear who should *not* be in a position to impose restraints: those who are not qualified to do so by virtue of scholarly training and accomplishment, including trustees, politicians, and donors. This principle was well established in a 1929 case at the University of Missouri investigated by the AAUP. There one faculty member was dismissed and another suspended after a student working under their supervision as part of a research project distributed to the student body a questionnaire about sexual mores that, in the words of the university president, was "bound to disturb the opinions of a large number of people." Among those disturbed were members of the university's Board of Curators, who concluded that the project was not only offensive—and likely to cause "harm or injury to the moral life of students"—but "from its very nature could not produce any scientifically valid conclusions nor any facts likely to be of substantial value." To this claim the AAUP's investigating committee responded, "the Board can express itself about the social expediency of an investigation and about other such general and public aspects of current scientific work. But it is presumptuous for a Board of Curators to make pronouncements about the scientific value of any investigation. Scientific investigations do proceed in all reputable universities in spite of differences of opinion about their validity. Scientific validity has never been established by any legal procedure or by the dictates of any board."[2]

The lesson of the case was, of course, that legitimate restraints on research can be established and policed only by the community of trained researchers itself. It was a lesson still lost in 2002 on the president of Mercer University, a Baptist institution in Macon, Georgia, who halted circulation of a similar survey of sex habits developed by a class under the leadership of a psychology professor and approved unanimously by the school's Institutional Review Board. The professor promptly left the school for a new, better-paid position elsewhere. Of the Mercer administration, he said, "They are willing to grant academic freedom only when people do what they want them to."[3]

Peer Review

Faculty regulation of research is accomplished mainly via systems of peer review. Under those systems, expertise is mobilized to pass judgment on whether research projects are worth funding or should be published. Difficult questions have been raised about the efficacy of much peer review and about its fairness. Charges of bias, back-stabbing, and back-scratching are recurrent. In fact, it may be impossible to always draw a clear line between proper and improper review. Yet, despite the system's flaws and a few outstanding cases of abuse, most of the time and in most instances it works well enough, no matter how vocal dissenters from review decisions may occasionally become.

Peer review is designed first and foremost to root out practices that no sensible person would deem worthy of protection by academic freedom, including plagiarism and research fraud. It does not always succeed even in this, however, as several embarrassing incidents from recent years in the sciences reveal. In 2013, three MIT graduate students created an algorithm to create fake scientific papers; as many as 120 papers generated by the program were published. Another 2013 hoax saw a scientific paper about fictional lichen published in several hundred journals.

Scientists, an editor of the *New England Journal of Medicine* observed in 1989, may be "intensely skeptical about the possibility of error, but totally trusting about the possibility of fraud."

"If you have an author who deliberately tries to mislead, it's surprisingly easy for them to do so," echoed the editor of the *Lancet* after a widely publicized study of hydroxychloroquine use in treatment of COVID-19 was retracted in June 2020 by the journal, which called the study "a fabrication." Another article on COVID-19 treatment using data from the same source was retracted the same day by the *New England Journal of Medicine*. The two journals are often ranked first and second in "impact factor" among general-interest medical journals. Their retractions highlighted growing strains in the peer review process in medicine and, to some extent, the sciences as a whole. One factor is the accelerated pace at which reviews now proceed. A second is the overburdening of potential peer reviewers. One epidemiologist reported that scientific journals "struggle to get good peer reviewers and try to do as well as they can, but the system is at risk of failing." These challenges facing peer review in the sciences threaten to imperil already fragile public faith in expert knowledge, a topic discussed further in chapter 8.

If peer review processes may occasionally become dangerously indulgent or insufficiently careful in their application of standards, more troubling may be the destructive influence of external pressures, especially if the research in question or the researcher under review is politically or otherwise controversial. In 2007, American Indian Studies professor Ward Churchill was dismissed from a tenured position at the University of Colorado after charges of plagiarism and other academic misconduct involving his scholarship were filed against him and accepted by a faculty committee. The violations were relatively minor and probably did not justify dismissal. More important, however, it is unlikely they would have been brought had Churchill not made widely publicized comments about the victims of the 9/11 attacks, prompting demands from politicians and others for his dismissal. Given that the committee judging his fitness was also inappropriately constituted, it is difficult to deny that the research misconduct of which Churchill was guilty served largely as a pretext for removing him for his controversial extramural speech.

In two celebrated cases involving historians, controversies over peer review and research fraud raised disturbing questions about the role of external pressures that implicate academic freedom. In 1981, David Abraham, then an assistant professor at Princeton, published an ambitious first book, *The Collapse of the Weimar Republic*, which employed Marxist methodology to argue that big business had played an important part in the Nazi rise to power. The book was reviewed favorably, but two senior historians, Henry Turner at Yale and Gerald Feldman at Berkeley (Feldman had previously written a positive prepublication peer review), began raising questions about Abraham's research. He acknowledged errors, which he would correct in a second edition, but contended—as did his defenders—that these did not fundamentally undermine his argument. He was denied tenure, and when he sought other employment Turner and Feldman tirelessly tracked his applications, regularly submitting unsolicited communications that warned against hiring him. When Abraham was under consideration for a library position in Israel, Feldman said that giving him such a post would be "like putting Dracula in charge of a blood bank." The two threatened to take their protests to boards of trustees, prompting complaints from members of search committees considering Abraham for a position. He eventually went to law school and became a distinguished law professor.

Abraham's critics argued that his was a case of serious academic misconduct and research fraud, properly exposed through processes of scholarly review and debate. His defenders saw it as a case of overzealous hounding of a junior scholar for what were mainly minor errors, conducted by more senior persecutors who were hardly disinterested. Turner, after all, confessed that were Abraham's work accurate, his own project on a similar topic would have to be abandoned. Feldman's graduate student was also working on related topics. Worse still, many believed the campaign against Abraham was motivated more by political discomfort with his conclusions and his avowed leftism than by concern for disciplinary standards. For many it served as a warning to young historians that to advance in the profession, it might be wise to steer clear of controversial topics or approaches.

In 2002, Emory University historian Michael Belleisles published *Arming America: The Origins of a National Gun Culture* to wide acclaim, with the book winning the prestigious Bancroft Prize. It argued, as Belleisles would later summarize, that "America's gun culture did not exist at its founding, but developed with the expansion of the gun industry, becoming fixed in our society with the Civil War." Gun rights advocates were incensed, and Belleisles received a slew of hate mail and online abuse. Serious historians also found some of his arguments troubling, and soon charges of faulty and fraudulent research mounted. Emory appointed a special committee of outside experts to review the charges. They called the work's treatment of probate sources "deeply flawed" after Belleisles was unable to provide them with all his research notes on that material because most had been destroyed when his office flooded. The committee concluded that the professor's "scholarly integrity is seriously in question." Belleisles disputed the findings, while correcting some errors, but resigned his position at Emory nonetheless. The Bancroft Prize was revoked and Belleisles became a bartender.

The controversy over the book centered on three paragraphs that discussed the probate records. After nearly two decades of silence, in 2019, Belleisles sat for an extensive interview in which he again defended his work, raising difficult questions about academic freedom in the Internet age. "Any work of history, I like to think, is going to contain a few errors which, in a spirit of goodwill, we should acknowledge, we should correct, and we should then move on with our research—to move closer to discovering the truth," he confessed.

I suspect that *Arming America* was subjected to the most excruciating scrutiny of any work of history in our lifetimes. Yet other than the probate records, I know of no significant errors uncovered. One can certainly disagree with my interpretation of particular materials. And I welcome that. . . .

So allow me to say that it is difficult to imagine the scale of the attack leveled on *Arming America*—I don't think that this could have been done to any book other than one on the topic of firearms. Members of the National Rifle Association launched a coordinated paragraph-by-paragraph search for errors. . . . Scholars who have examined the battle over *Arming America* . . . generally seem to believe that the controversy was both an indication of the NRA expanding its power to foreclose research into America's gun culture, an influence that extended [to ending] all gun research by the CDC and the NIH; and as the first use of methods that would later be identified as swiftboating. . . . The controversy also saw the appearance of a type of online conduct that is now known as trolling. . . .

Arming America was published about a particular topic at a particular time in our history, which opened it up to the possibility of denial of scholarship in a way that had never been experienced before. It is because it's the subject of guns that it attracted this attention—and, because . . . people were not yet aware of the way in which the Web and its ancillaries [could] provide . . . a terrible weapon in the hands of the willfully ignorant. . . . If we could somehow extract *Arming America* from the politically motivated criticisms, what you would see would be a work of scholarship which has flaws like any other work of scholarship, that has a specific argument like any other legitimate work of scholarship, and that is open to debate like any other legitimate work of scholarship.[4]

The point here is not to rehabilitate Belleisles or his book, but to suggest how a politically polarized environment and the power of the internet can pose formidable challenges to peer review processes in ways that can endanger academic freedom.

Recent efforts to compel the retraction of controversial studies via petition campaigns, sometimes promoted or joined by scholars with contrary views, are another troubling phenomenon. "Petitions are instruments of pressure; they're not instruments of persuasion, argument or evidence," explained Canadian philosophy professor Mark Mercer. As one physicist noted, "Just because a thousand voices say the same thing, that doesn't make it right. You can end up in scenarios where a scientific orthodoxy develops, and publishing material that supports that kind of thinking and its main proponents becomes much easier than going against the stream." Nonetheless, as Carl Sagan was fond of pointing out, "extraordinary claims require extraordinary evidence." Researchers whose work challenges existing orthodoxies or which may offend some readers should therefore expect to be held to rigorous standards.[5]

Institutional Review Boards

In the 1929 Missouri case, the Board of Curators charged the professors with pursuing research that would cause moral harm. The charge was ridiculous, but it is undeniable that some kinds of research may indeed cause harm if not controlled. Universities impose health and safety regulations on laboratories, for example, all the time; these hardly constitute a restraint on the academic freedom of researchers who work there. In the wake of revelations about the notorious Tuskegee syphilis experiment—in which, over a forty-year span, doctors at the US Public Health Service left unsuspecting African-American men with syphilis untreated as researchers observed the disease's progress—Congress passed the National Research Act of 1974. The act mandated colleges and universities to establish Institutional Review Boards

(IRBs), composed largely of faculty members, to review and approve all federally funded research on human subjects and ensure that risks to subjects be balanced by potential benefits to society and that selection of subjects present a fair or just distribution of risks and benefits to eligible participants. Most universities also employ IRBs in screening nonfederally funded human subjects research.

IRBs represent a peculiar kind of peer review, insofar as they are obligated to conform to policies defined by the government and not by scholars themselves. Critics therefore charge that IRBs pose a threat to academic freedom, especially in the social sciences. A once-modest safety control, many contend, has grown into thousands of independently operating ethical review boards implementing increasingly complex regulations, whose power has expanded alarmingly over time, with little control or guidance. Some IRBs function as de facto representatives of a university's concerns not only about health and safety but also about liability, bad publicity, and political exposure, which can be especially problematic for social scientists conducting research on controversial subjects like race or sexuality. Moreover, especially in larger institutions, much of the work of IRBs is now conducted by administrative staff who may "judge applications not as peer reviewers or ethicists but as bureaucrats." In science and medicine, in particular, much of their work may even be outsourced to private for-profit IRBs.[6]

In 1999 and 2000, AAUP staff members met with representatives from a variety of social science organizations to assess how the system was affecting social science research. A resulting report offered recommendations for improvement, but also concluded that "a university's effort to ensure that all researchers comply with its human-subject regulations does not offend academic freedom." Nonetheless, the report added, "there is the possibility . . . that the specific rules adopted by the government or a university to protect human subjects could abridge academic freedom." A subsequent 2006 report by a subcommittee of Committee A found "the fact that research on human subjects must obtain IRB approval whether or not it imposes a serious risk of harm on its subjects" to be "deeply troublesome." The report recommended "that research on autonomous adults whose methodology consists entirely in collecting data by surveys, conducting interviews, or observing behavior in public places, be exempt from the requirement of IRB review." The Obama administration promulgated reforms designed to facilitate research on biospecimens and to free oral historians and journalists from IRB jurisdiction, but implementation has been uneven.[7] The appropriate balance between protection of human subjects and academic freedom remains in dispute.

Freedom to Publish and Classified Research

The right of professors not only to conduct research freely but also freely to publish the results was tested in 1918, when the chancellor of the University of Montana, after consultation with the governor, forbade an economics professor from publishing work on taxation of the state's mining industry that was politically embarrassing. When the professor published it anyway, he was suspended. A faculty committee, however, concluded that the chancellor's order was "an unsound educational policy." If implemented, they argued, "no member of the faculty may discuss any of the public questions under consideration." Implicitly echoing the 1915 *Declaration*'s distinction between faculty as employees and faculty as appointees, the committee distinguished work conducted by an employee of a business from that conducted by a faculty member. "Some hold the opinion," the committee argued,

> that as a railroad president may pigeon-hole the report of an engineer . . . or as a capitalist may keep in his desk a report of any employee who has investigated a proposed project, so may the Chancellor withhold temporarily or permanently any report

which may be prepared by faculty members, and which he may think should not be divulged.

The situations are not analogous. There is a vast difference between a private trust and a public trust. The University belongs in the service of the people of the state. The Chancellor should not even claim the right or privilege of representing the people of the state. He should not say what the people shall or shall not hear or be told.

This distinction between public and private interest suggests that the work of university researchers must be publicly available, unlike much paid work for government agencies or in private industry. In those spheres research results have not generally been controlled by researchers themselves and can be, and often are, kept secret. Research universities, by contrast, were conceived of as a public good, where unfettered investigation pushes new boundaries with results readily available to the public. During World War II, however, significant numbers of university scholars, such as Berkeley physicist J. Robert Oppenheimer, signed up for classified government research in the Manhattan Project and similar efforts in which both the conduct and results of their classified work were subject to close supervision and extensive censorship. As the hot war against the Axis gave way to the Cold War against Communism, what had been exceptional became ever more commonplace, and the public/private distinction drawn by the Montana committee grew a good deal hazier.

Consider this from Kate Brown, a historian of science at the Massachusetts Institute of Technology:

From the end of World War II until the 1970s, federal grants paid for 70 percent of university research. The largest federal donors were the Department of Defense, the US Atomic Energy Agency, and a dozen federal security agencies. Historian Peter Galison estimated in 2004 that the volume of classified research surpassed open literature in American libraries by five to ten times. Put another way, for every article published by American academics in open journals, five to ten articles were filed in sealed repositories available only to the 4 million Americans with security clearances. Often, the same researchers penned both open and classified work.

This change has not been without consequence. According to Brown, extensive classification—largely unjustified, she charges—of research in health physics for decades prevented accurate assessment of the disastrous health consequences of the nuclear accident at Chernobyl. In that field "a closed circle of knowledge . . . has had a major impact on our abilities to assess and respond to both nuclear emergencies and quotidian radioactive contamination."[8]

Classified research and all research that cannot be published is inappropriate on a college or university campus. Although academic freedom leaves it to faculty members to control what to do—or not to do—with the results of their investigations, it does *not* entitle faculty members to sign away their freedom to disseminate research results. In 1967, referring specifically to contracts between individual scholars or universities and the CIA, the annual meeting of the AAUP resolved that "all secret arrangements entered into by academic institutions or individuals in an academic capacity threaten the integrity of the academic community." That concern was reaffirmed in a second resolution the following year. In 1983, the AAUP issued a report, *The Enlargement of the Classified Information System*, which addressed a Reagan administration executive order that "significantly abridges academic freedom beyond the needs of national security." The report observed that secrecy in research not only restricts public knowledge, it also yields "the bleak prospect of academic researchers who are walled-off from each other," thereby hampering "the exchange of ideas and constructive criticism." In a 2003 statement titled *Academic Freedom and National Security in a Time of Crisis*, the association again affirmed that "secrecy, an inescapable element of classified research, is fundamentally incompatible with freedom of inquiry and freedom of expression."

National security has also been used at times to justify other potentially improper restraints on freedom of research. These include federal laws that require the licensing of certain exports, including research results, and increased barriers to entry into the United States by foreign scholars. An amicus brief filed by seventeen private research universities in opposition to the Trump administration's ban on immigration from certain countries argued that "American laboratories, which are a major driver of our economy, depend on the ability to attract the best trainees and postdoctoral fellows from around the world, as well as the collaboration of foreign scientists in areas of science that have no defense or security implications."

In recent decades, concerns about the growth of China's commercial and political strength have led to often unfounded charges that Chinese scholars and scholars of Chinese descent have engaged in espionage under the cover of legitimate research. The Committee of 100, a nonprofit organization of prominent Chinese-Americans, has charged that "the loyalties of Chinese Americans are being unfairly questioned, and the community is being severely maligned by overreaching prosecutions and rush to judgment." As a 2017 report by the AAUP acknowledged, "there are certainly instances in which foreign governments or corporations have violated both national security and intellectual property rights of Americans." But "the conflation of commercial interest and national security" by the US government has too often led to careless actions that threaten international scientific exchange and freedom of research. A notorious example was the case of Temple University professor of physics Xiaoxing Xi, a naturalized American citizen. In 2015, Professor Xi was arrested by the FBI at gunpoint and charged with wire fraud, stemming from emails sent to scientists in China about a collaboration involving a thin-film deposition mechanism that the government charged was a classified device called a pocket heater. The charges were eventually dropped, after experts demonstrated that the devices Xi had discussed with Chinese colleagues did not include a pocket heater and the exchanges posed no threat to US interests.[9]

In 2019, the National Science Foundation charged JASON, an independent group of elite scientists that advises the US government on matters of science and technology, to produce a report addressing concern "that the openness of our academic fundamental research ecosystem is being taken advantage of by other countries." The report concluded that "many of the problems of foreign influence that have been identified are ones that can be addressed within the framework of research integrity, and that the benefits of openness in research and of the inclusion of talented foreign researchers dictate against measures that would wall off particular areas of fundamental research." JASON found "problems with respect to research transparency, lack of reciprocity in collaborations and consortia, and reporting of commitments and potential conflicts of interest," but acknowledged that "the scale and scope of the problem remain poorly defined." The report recommended expanded "education and training in scientific ethics." It urged the NSF to "make clear that fundamental research should remain unrestricted to the fullest extent possible, and to discourage the use of new C[ontrolled] U[nclassified] I[nformation] definitions."[10]

Questions about undue Chinese influence have also been raised with respect to the Confucius Institutes, Chinese-language and cultural centers funded by the Chinese government and established at some American and Canadian universities. In 2014, the AAUP warned that these institutes can "function as an arm of the Chinese state and are allowed to ignore academic freedom" since their curricula and faculty fall under the supervision of a Chinese state agency. Agreements establishing the institutes generally contain "nondisclosure clauses and unacceptable concessions to the political aims and practices of the government of China." More recently, the US government weighed in, with the

State Department in August 2020 branding the Confucius Institute US Center a "foreign mission" of the Chinese government and "an entity advancing Beijing's global propaganda and malign influence campaign on US campuses and K-12 classrooms." This went well beyond the AAUP's concerns about restrictions on academic freedom and faculty control of research and curriculum, however.[11]

Academy-Industry Relationships

Between 1970 and 2000 the share of university research funding from private industry tripled in value. According to the National Science Foundation, in 2009 some institutions received anywhere from 12 to 50 percent of their research budgets from private industry sources. Funding is concentrated in fields like medicine, biology, chemistry, engineering, and agriculture. In recent years, private funding has also expanded in economics and business, as well as elsewhere in the social sciences and even the humanities, often from politically motivated conservative and libertarian sources, about which more shortly.

As early as 1951, sociologist C. Wright Mills noted the emergence in academia of "the new entrepreneur," whose career had become "dependent upon the traits of the go-getter in business and the manager in the corporation," and whose research may "become more directly an appendage of the larger managerial demiurge."[12] In 2014, the AAUP published a book-length report, *Recommended Principles to Guide Academy-Industry Relationships*, which observed that in addition to obtaining private research funding, faculty members "frequently engage with outside companies in other ways as well. Many faculty . . . consult for private companies and sit on their boards." As many colleges and universities now function more like businesses themselves, some individual faculty members have responded by becoming "entrepreneurial" participants in what has been called "academic capitalism." Sheila Slaughter has cautioned that "as segments of the professoriate align themselves with the market and make great personal gains from the synergy between their university work and their corporate endeavors, their claims about the need for buffers from external pressures ring less true, undermining their historic stance as disinterested scientists and experts, which is the foundation on which the claim of academic freedom rests." Public disclosure of funding sources is at best uneven, often making it difficult to distinguish between academic research and efforts that, for all intents and purposes, more closely resemble work "made for hire." "Academic freedom does not entitle faculty members to ignore financial conflicts of interest," the 2014 report declared. It also "does not guarantee faculty members the freedom to take money regardless of the conditions attached."[13]

Faculty research was significantly impacted by the passage in 1980 of the Bayh-Dole Act, which established a uniform policy with regard to intellectual property rights in federally funded university research. Bayh-Dole "did not mandate either that universities own, or have a first right to own, inventions made with federal support." The act did, however, direct "universities to require their research personnel to make a written agreement to protect the government's interest in any inventions they may make." Over the next thirty years, universities came to claim that Bayh-Dole granted the institution and not individual investigators exclusive rights to the products of federally supported research on campus. In 2011, in the case of *Board of Trustees of Leland Stanford Junior University v. Roche Molecular Systems, Inc.,* the US Supreme Court disagreed. Siding with arguments presented in an amicus brief by the AAUP, the Court ruled that the act did not vest title to inventions by faculty members in their university employers, nor did it require faculty to assign their intellectual property rights to their universities. This was an important victory for the academic freedom to publish, but in response some research universities now compel newly hired faculty members to sign over these rights in advance, as either a condition of university support for research or a condition of employment itself, a practice called "present assignment." Sometimes they claim falsely that this is "required" by *Stanford v. Roche.* In several instances, universities have sought to amend existing faculty contracts to add such a provision, in at least one case threatening to withhold all institutional research support if professors fail to comply.[14]

Whether applied to patentable inventions or material subject to copyright protection, the basic principle is the same. As the AAUP's 1999 *Statement on Copyright* put it with regard to all forms of faculty research, "the faculty member rather than the institution determines the subject matter, the intellectual approach and direction and the conclusions." Giving an institution control over the "dissemination of the work" is "deeply inconsistent with fundamental principles of academic freedom." Sadly, these principles are seriously eroding. "Much of what can be assigned as intellectual property in higher education is being claimed by its institutions, with the interests of the public being harmed in the process," one prominent legal scholar claims. "Most of the developments in university research and invention policies over the past thirty years have significantly limited or even ended opportunities for faculty investigators and inventors to decide the disposition of their research results and instructional materials, whether prepared for their colleagues, for a sponsor of research, for industry, or for the classroom," the AAUP's *Academy-Industry* report observed. "Faculty with little bargaining power, including PhDs in their first jobs, are particularly vulnerable to pressure to sign away their invention rights, possibly for their entire careers."[15]

Faculty in disciplines where the likelihood of invention is slight may believe these developments will have little or no impact on them. But if university administrators can control the products of patentable research, why not copyrightable materials as well? That was certainly the aspiration of the Montana chancellor a century ago. He sought control in order to silence a politically risky study. Today's managers seek instead to capture earnings from faculty work as part of a never-ending (and often vain) search for revenue. So imagine the temptation should the movie rights to an English professor's best-selling novel sell for millions.

Open Access

If classified research and private funding restrictions endanger academic freedom, issues also arise with access to research published in scholarly journals. While the digital world has offered great promise to make information widely accessible, journal publishers and other commercial forces have restricted much research behind paywalls and through licensing agreements. Rising subscription costs also place inordinate burdens on the availability of research products, including the ability of underfunded college and university libraries to pay for them.

One response to this situation has been the open access movement, which seeks to reduce the influence of publishers and open doors to free sharing of research results. It encourages faculty members to publish in journals that do not require payment, either via subscription or for individual articles, to access what they publish. But some open access journals avoid peer review; others may be deemed predatory. Moreover, as one critic noted, "while it's great in theory that open access has removed price barriers for some consumers, in fact the price barriers are shifting to the author side. In other words, for the most part open access moves the financing of scholarly publishing from consumer to author." To avoid such problems, a growing number of colleges and universities now ask their faculty members to place research products in an open-access site maintained by the institution in addition to their publication in journals. For example, the University of California requires its faculty members to grant "a nonexclusive, irrevocable, worldwide license to exercise any and all rights under copyright relating to each of his or her scholarly articles, in any medium, and to authorize others to do the same, for the purpose of making their articles widely and freely available in an open access repository."[16]

The AAUP's *Statement on Copyright* affirmed that "it has been the prevailing academic practice to treat the faculty member as the copyright owner of works that are created independently and at the faculty member's own initiative for traditional academic purposes." It is therefore a violation of academic freedom for an institution to mandate that members of its faculty cede any rights under copyright law, including in pursuit of open access. However, faculty members who wish to participate in such arrangements should be free to do so, which is why most institutions that have adopted such policies, including the University of California, appropriately provide opportunities to "opt out" or receive a waiver. Whether that is sufficient protection, however, may not always be clear.

Donors

Politically motivated donors constitute one group unqualified to pass judgment on the validity of faculty research or to influence its results and dissemination. In recent decades such donors have overwhelmingly come from conservative and libertarian circles, most famously the donor network created by oilman Charles Koch and his foundation. These donors have aggressively sought to counter what they perceive as an overwhelmingly leftist faculty bias, which allegedly hides behind the banner of academic freedom. "Academic freedom," one such donor group declared, "is not only about protection against administrative intrusion into the objective inquiry of faculty but also about the faculty evolving over time into a special interest group that limits the range of ideas expressed on campus." In response to such concerns, these donors employ their philanthropy to promote an ideological and political agenda as part of an ambitious and coordinated strategy aimed, critics charge, less at supporting scholarship and more toward leveraging influence in higher education for broader political ends.[17]

In 2016, Koch interests alone awarded $50 million in grants to some 249 institutions. George Mason University, a public institution in Virginia, has been the biggest beneficiary of Koch largesse, much of which has gone to the creation and promotion of politically defined centers and institutes. Such centers, at George Mason and elsewhere, no matter their sponsors, may resemble what the 1915 *Declaration* called a "proprietary school or college designed for the propagation of specific doctrines prescribed by those who have furnished its endowment" and which therefore "should not be permitted to sail under false colors. Genuine boldness and thoroughness of inquiry, and freedom of speech, are scarcely reconcilable with the prescribed inculcation of a particular opinion upon a controverted question."[18]

Representatives of Koch interests often participate on the boards of these entities, at times exerting undue influence on faculty hiring and promotion decisions. In 2016, the Charles Koch Foundation gave George Mason's law school $10 million, which was paired with a $20 million donation from an anonymous donor affiliated with the conservative Federalist Society, resulting in the school's renaming in honor of the late Justice Antonin Scalia. University leaders assured a skeptical faculty senate, which had expressed "deep concern" about the confidential terms of the donor agreements, that nothing was untoward. But documents released in response to a Freedom of Information Act request revealed that the Federalist Society had been inappropriately influencing faculty hiring and student placement, redirecting scholarship money to favored programs, and even reorienting the school's judicial law clerk programs to place law students associated with the society in influential clerkships. At Florida State University, a faculty investigation found that Koch gifts to the economics department violated principles of academic freedom and shared governance, amounting to a "two-fold conflict of interest" executed by "administrative dictate," producing an "atmosphere of intimidation."

The potentially malign influence of politically motivated donors can extend beyond research to impact the overall atmosphere for free expression and hence academic freedom on a campus. One illustration came in June 2020, when a technical college affiliated with Wichita State University, in a concession to student and faculty criticism, dropped plans for a virtual commencement address by Ivanka Trump. In a compromise arranged by the school's president, her recorded remarks were simply included as one in a menu of choices. In response, Koch Industries, headquartered in Wichita, threatened to withdraw its support for the university. Koch has reportedly given or pledged some $15 million to WSU. In addition, the Koch foundation has committed $3.6 million to the university's Institute for the Study of Economic Growth, a center devoted to promoting Koch's libertarian ideas. Another corporate donor allied with Koch called on the institution's Board of Regents to fire the president. The Wichita State board held a closed-door session while students rallied and circulated a petition in support of the president. After meeting for four hours, the board issued a statement supporting "freedom of speech and diversity and inclusion." Koch Industries then sought to recast the company's objections, denying that they had sought the president's ouster. "We object to speaker disinvitations," a statement declared. But a professor who wrote an open letter opposing the Trump address pointed out that "any student who wants to opt-in and hear Ivanka Trump's speech can. It wasn't cancelled, or censored. . . . The real peril is these business partnerships. They think they own the school. That's the First Amendment issue," she said. "The political pressure that wealthy donors exert on universities rarely gets aired so publicly," commented *New Yorker* writer Jane Mayer.[19]

These and numerous other instances in which the Koch foundation or its allies abused faculty rights have led to faculty protests and the formation of a largely student-inspired UnKoch My Campus movement. In response, the Charles Koch Foundation altered the terms of its giving, pledging no longer to interfere in decisions appropriately under faculty purview and vowing to respect academic freedom. Critics remain skeptical. But recipients of Koch funding may have legitimate grounds to complain that the UnKoch movement can threaten their academic freedom. Almost uniformly, they claim that conservative funders have never interfered with their work. "I was doing this research, and I had this vision and mission" before the Koch Foundation offered money, said one grant recipient.

This shouldn't come as much of a surprise. Donors naturally tend to donate to work that meets with their approval. And while it is totally improper for a donor to demand a predetermined outcome to research being funded, there is little improper in providing support for favored methodologies, hypotheses, and research agendas. Indeed, it would be foolish, especially in our politically polarized era, to assume that only money from the Right will be problematic. "Shouldn't we be concerned about anyone who is funding any academic research centers on political and social subjects, no matter their ideological direction?" asked one journalist. The outsized influence of the Bill and Melinda Gates Foundation on medical research has also come under criticism, especially its funding of the University of Washington's quasi-independent Institute for Health Metrics and Evaluation, which has been called a "monopoly . . . with a constellation of high-profile allies that have made it too big to peer review."[20]

Critics of the content of research conducted by externally funded and ideologically motivated research centers are well within their rights to voice criticisms of the research and publications that come out of those centers and to subject them to scrutiny. But insofar as academic freedom is concerned, the issue is not so much the viewpoints being advanced or the quality of the scholarship, but whether donor funding agreements are fully transparent, the university maintains its autonomy, and the faculty's rights to both academic freedom and collective control of research efforts are properly upheld. Experience suggests that these criteria may be observed less often than they are violated.

Confidentiality of Research Materials

Another threat to freedom of research takes the form of efforts by politically motivated outsiders to "expose" the confidential research correspondence of scholars they wish to discredit. In 2009, climate change deniers hacked into a British university server and stole thousands of email messages exchanged by climate scientists. Selectively released and quoted, they could be made to appear as if the scientists were conspiring to improperly manipulate data and suppress critics. The resulting brouhaha became known as Climategate. At least eight committees investigated the allegations, however, finding no evidence of fraud or scientific misconduct. In April 2010, the attorney general of Virginia demanded emails and a variety of other materials and documents relating to Michael Mann, a climate scientist who was a faculty member at the University of Virginia until 2005, when he left for Pennsylvania State University. Professor Mann was one of the scientists whose emails were hacked in Climategate. In 2012, the Virginia Supreme Court rejected the effort, concluding that the law did not grant the attorney general authority to make the request. That led to several other cases in which private groups made similar demands in Virginia and elsewhere. The effort failed in Virginia, but in Arizona, after extended litigation, the state Supreme Court denied motions by the Arizona Board of Regents for stays of the release of emails of two climate scientists in response to a 2011 public records law request by a climate change denial group.

An ongoing analysis of protections for research materials by the Climate Science Legal Defense Fund has found that "legal protections for scientific research materials vary widely in the United States, leaving scientists and universities vulnerable to malicious open records requests and endangering the scientific endeavor." The report added, "Bad-faith open records requests damage science in many ways, from discouraging frank conversations to providing opportunities for hostile actors to misconstrue phrases, including scientific jargon, and use these to mislead or confuse the public."[21] In an amicus brief submitted in the Arizona case, the AAUP argued that "academic freedom is a central factor to protect the state's interest in ensuring faculty ability to engage in open and uninhibited research and collaboration with colleagues. Where public records requests seek prepublication communications and other unpublished academic research materials . . . compelled disclosure would have a severe chilling effect on intellectual debate among researchers and scientists."

Research and the Erosion of Tenure

As part of the ongoing erosion of the tenure system and the dramatic increase in hiring of faculty on limited-term contracts, there has been a significant growth in full-time research faculty employed on a contingent basis, most visibly in medical schools and STEM disciplines. Often such research faculty must raise money to support their own salaries. Because they are perpetually hustling for funding, such academic "entrepreneurs" may find themselves compelled to accept conditions that violate academic freedom or even to embrace such violations. More widespread is the growing use and abuse of postdocs, to be discussed in chapter 5.

The dangers for academic freedom of research appointments without protections of tenure may be seen most vividly in the case of hydrologist Ivor van Heerden, at Louisiana State University. For years, his work on coastal erosion and hurricane- and flood-related issues brought him public prominence, consistently favorable evaluations, and repeated reappointment to his non-tenure-track position. In 2005, Hurricane Katrina heightened van Heerden's profile, to the initial delight of LSU administrators. Their attitude quickly changed, however, after he found that a main cause of flooding and resulting loss of lives was structural failure of the levees overseen by the US Army Corps of Engineers. Administrators had hoped to cooperate with and gain support from the Corps in recovery projects, so they were not happy to see these findings. They took steps to restrain van Heerden's public activities and to distance LSU from those activities, and, eventually, they denied van Heerden further appointment. The AAUP investigated, concluding that even though van Heerden was not eligible for tenure, LSU had still improperly denied him due process, to which he was entitled through length of service. The university also violated his academic freedom by denying him reappointment largely in retaliation for his dissent from the prevailing LSU stance on the levees and by restricting the nature of the research he could conduct. Van Heerden filed a wrongful termination suit and was eventually awarded $435,000.[22]

Artistic Expression

Before concluding this discussion of academic freedom in research and the publication of results, it is necessary to turn to an area in which the connection to research may appear vague: artistic expression. Clearly, law professors may write novels; historians may create paintings; and mathematicians may perform music,[23] but when they do so, it is virtually always independent of their teaching and research responsibilities. Hence, should such efforts provoke controversy, they merit protection as forms of extramural expression. But universities regularly include departments in which the production of creative work is central to the department's mission, including departments of art, music, theater, dance, or creative writing. Should works of imagination created by the faculty of such programs be considered "research" and hence protected by academic freedom?

This has not always been clear, even to the faculty in these programs. In 1971, the modernist composer Charles Wuorinen was denied tenure in the Music Department at Columbia just a year after winning a Pulitzer Prize. A number of factors were apparently at play, but one issue was whether musical composition could count as "research" in a department committed more to musicology: the study of music as an academic subject as distinct from training in performance or composition.

In the 1930s, the AAUP investigated the non-reappointment of an English professor because his novel was said to upset the college dean. The investigation report called the case a matter of "improper restriction of literary freedom," concluding that "it seems a sound proposition that a teacher who is a creative writer should have complete freedom of expression." In 1960, the AAUP investigated a case in which another English professor was dismissed after his novel was deemed by a local book club "the filthiest book they had ever read." Again, the AAUP concluded that the case involved violation of "the responsible exercise of academic freedom." But, Finkin and Post have asked, on what grounds may we appeal in such cases to academic freedom? Were the novels in question a variety of scholarly "research" or were they extramural expression? In fact, Finkin and Post have argued that, even today, academic freedom in the production and teaching of artistic work "has not yet been adequately theorized."[24]

It is not apparent, however, to what extent further theorizing is needed. In 1990, the AAUP, the American Council on Education, the Association of Governing Boards of Universities and Colleges, and the Wolf Trap Foundation issued a statement titled *Academic Freedom and Artistic Expression*. The statement proposed that "academic freedom in the creation and presentation of works in the visual and the performing arts, by ensuring greater opportunity for imaginative exploration and expression, best serves the public and the academy." It continued, "Faculty members and students engaged in the creation and presentation of works of the visual and performing arts are as much engaged in pursuing the mission of the college or university as are those who write, teach, and study in other academic disciplines. . . . Artistic expression in the classroom, the studio, and the workshop therefore merits the same assurance of academic freedom that is accorded to other scholarly and teaching activities."[25]

This statement seems strong enough. Whether it means that faculty work in this area should be counted as research or as extramural expression is largely up to individual faculties to decide as they develop and revise evaluation standards for hiring, tenure, promotion, reappointment, or other forms of recognition or reward. Had Columbia made explicit that Wuorinen's responsibility was to produce research *about* music, not to produce music itself, his dismissal would be unobjectionable, at least on academic freedom grounds. But if a school or department defines the teaching or research requirements of faculty in the arts to include the actual practice of their art, as opposed only to its study, then such works merit protection by academic freedom as much as any other work of research. Colleges and universities are free to decide whether to have an English department that includes or does not include creative writing. Similarly they may decide to support a theater department, whether or not it offers instruction in acting or produces plays. But if a college or university recognizes creative artistic expression as part of a faculty work assignment, expressive works in the arts by such faculty members should then be recognized as scholarship equivalent to research and protected by academic freedom. Similarly, such work may also be part of or relevant to a faculty member's role as a teacher, which is the topic of the next chapter.

Chapter 3

Teaching

❝It is scarcely open to question that freedom of utterance is as important to the teacher as it is to the investigator," the 1915 *Declaration* proclaimed. It stands to reason that if scholars are free to disseminate the results of their research to the public, they surely must be free to do so to their students. But all faculty who teach do not conduct research, and even those who do so frequently teach material removed from their own scholarly expertise. Therefore, the authors of the 1915 *Declaration* did not found their support for freedom in the classroom on its connection with the freedom to conduct research. Instead, they wrote:

> No man can be a successful teacher unless he enjoys the respect of his students, and their confidence in his intellectual integrity. It is clear, however, that this confidence will be impaired if there is suspicion on the part of the student that the teacher is not expressing himself fully or frankly, or that college and university teachers in general are a repressed and intimidated class who dare not speak with that candor and courage which youth always demands in those whom it is to esteem. The average student is a discerning observer, who soon takes the measure of his instructor. It is not

only the character of the instruction but also the character of the instructor that counts; and if the student has reason to believe that the instructor is not true to himself, the virtue of the instruction as an educative force is incalculably diminished. There must be in the mind of the teacher no mental reservation. He must give the student the best of what he has and what he is.

This was not to deny that college and university instructors should, as much as practicable, be knowledgeable and even, where possible, fully expert in the subjects they teach. But it was to recognize that the purpose of higher education is only secondarily the conveyance of information or transmission of dogmas. Its principal purpose, as Finkin and Post put it, is "to instill in students the mature independence of mind that characterizes successful adulthood." Such independence is "an active virtue, not a passive one," best "acquired through emulation." If their instructors are not free to practice and model such intellectual independence, students will be incapable of learning to exercise it themselves.[1]

The 1915 *Declaration,* however, acknowledged "certain special restraints" on the faculty's obligation to exercise and model independence of mind in the classroom. For many "immature students," the *Declaration* contended, "character is not yet fully formed." Hence, for these students "it may reasonably be expected that the instructor will present scientific truth with discretion, that he will introduce the student to new conceptions gradually, with some consideration for the student's preconceptions and traditions and with due regard to character building." Today this sentiment reads as dated deference to the principle of *in loco parentis* and an uncharacteristic concession to popular sentiment, although perhaps echoed in recent years by expressed fears that students may be made uncomfortable, even harmed, by a "hostile learning environment," about which more shortly.

As with freedom of research, the faculty's freedom in the classroom cannot be properly understood apart from its collective authority over the curriculum—as a whole, in a specific degree program, or even in a single course. This is manifested in a variety of concrete ways, as we shall see, but first it will be useful to address four common contemporary arguments for the contention that academic freedom in the classroom is being abused. These were addressed in a 2007 report by the AAUP's Committee A, titled *Freedom in the Classroom.* They are charges that "(1) instructors 'indoctrinate' rather than educate; (2) instructors fail fairly to present conflicting views on contentious subjects, thereby depriving students of educationally essential 'diversity' or 'balance'; (3) instructors are intolerant of students' religious, political, or socioeconomic views, thereby creating a hostile atmosphere inimical to learning; and (4) instructors persistently interject material, especially of a political or ideological character, irrelevant to the subject of instruction."[2]

Education, Not Indoctrination

Central to the rationale for freedom in teaching offered by the 1915 *Declaration* is that professors must educate, not indoctrinate students. But the line between the two cannot always be drawn precisely and without reference to applicable disciplinary principles. Can the presentation of essential factual information or foundational principles amount to indoctrination? Standard mathematical theorems are not debatable, but interpretation of a work of literature may well be. "It is not indoctrination for professors to expect students to comprehend ideas and apply knowledge that is accepted within a relevant discipline," *Freedom in the Classroom* states. Instruction is not indoctrination when, as the AAUP's first president, the philosopher John Dewey, pointed out, ideas and methods are largely uncontested. But it is an abuse of academic freedom, Dewey rightly believed, for an instructor to "promulgate *as truth* ideas or opinions which have *not* been tested," that is, propositions that have not been generally accepted as true within the relevant discipline. "Dewey's point," *Freedom in the Classroom* suggests, is "that indoctrination occurs whenever an instructor insists that students accept *as truth* propositions that are in fact professionally contestable . . . without allowing students to challenge their validity or advance alternative understandings."

In 1965, the AAUP investigated a case of an openly Marxist sociologist at Adelphi University, whose views were known to and tolerated by both his departmental colleagues and the university's administration. He was suspended, however, when he posed multiple-choice questions on a midterm exam that the investigating committee would deem "thoroughly unprofessional—badly drafted, ambiguous, tendentious, and prejudicial." The questions were inappropriate because their answers were based on acceptance as unquestioned truth of Marxist doctrines not collectively accepted as such in the academy, and the multiple-choice framework provided no opportunity for expressing dissent. Nonetheless, the committee did not approve the scholar's suspension because, if academic freedom is understood to be a collective right, its report found, the department's laissez-faire approach to the curriculum had given him "good reason to think" such questions might be "perfectly acceptable." The committee concluded that the professor had acted "in ways that were far from professional, as most academics would interpret professionalism. But this raises the question of professional standards at Adelphi."[3]

This does not mean, of course, that instructors cannot themselves assert with vigor viewpoints that remain controversial. Indeed, they must be free to do so because to engage in forceful argument and debate is essential to the educational mission and hence to academic freedom. It is only "when instructors assert such propositions in ways that prevent students from expressing disagreement" or from asking probing questions that indoctrination occurs. Moreover, "if an instructor has formed an opinion on a controversial question in adherence to scholarly standards of professional care, it is as much an exercise of academic freedom to test those opinions before students as it is to present them to the public at large."

"The fundamental point is that freedom in the classroom applies as much to controversial opinions as to studied agnosticism. So long as opinion and interpretation are not advanced and insisted upon as dogmatic truth, the style of presentation should be at the discretion of the instructor." But this freedom again cannot be the unfettered freedom of the individual instructor to promulgate ideas in total disregard for either disciplinary consensus or recognized dissenting trends within relevant scholarship.

Balance

If instructors are to introduce controversial ideas, critics contend, they must do so in a "balanced" manner. Teachers can inject bias, the argument goes, if they fail to present opposing views or give students a full accounting of the range of scholarly and popular opinion on a given topic. Although instructors must follow curricular guidelines approved by the larger faculty, freedom in the classroom affords "wide latitude to decide how to approach a subject, how best to present and explore the material, and so forth." Teachers are not obliged to strive for some abstract and impractical ideal of "neutrality." To demand that all interpretations must be presented is to demand the impossible because "there is always a potentially infinite number of competing perspectives that can arguably be deemed relevant" to a given subject.

Such a demand would also run counter to the instructor's accountability to disciplinary and professional standards. Those who call for balance seek "equal time" for viewpoints and theories that are most often grounded not in academic disputes but in political or cultural debates. Such, for instance, is the demand that evolutionary theory be "balanced" by creationism or climate science by climate change denial. Yet "the whole point of academic freedom is to insulate professional judgment from this kind of crude political control."[4] To require political neutrality and balance in the classroom—or to require that politics be expunged from the classroom entirely—is to require professors to be continually on the lookout for ideas that may have political salience, to sniff them out, so to speak, so they may either be suppressed or "balanced." Clearly such an approach would not only stifle classroom discussions but also undermine the development of the "mature independence of mind" that is the very purpose of higher education. It would lead, for all intents and purposes, to ruinous self-censorship.

"The duty of an academic instructor," the 1915 *Declaration* declared, is to provide "a genuine intellectual awakening and to arouse in [students] a keen desire to reach personally verified conclusions upon all questions of general concernment to mankind, or of special significance for their own time." To fulfill that duty, instructors must not so much offer balance as variety. This is another reason why academic freedom in the classroom is best conceived as a collective freedom of the faculty and not the individual right of the instructor. For if the college or university is to fulfill its mission, it must strive to ensure that in the course of their education students are exposed to many differing theoretical and pedagogical approaches. The *Declaration* quoted a college president of the time, who wrote that instructors may be forgiven "the occasional error of . . . doctrine" because "it is better for students to think about heresies than not to think at all; better for them to climb new trails, and stumble over error if need be, than to ride forever in upholstered ease in the overcrowded highway. It is a primary duty of a teacher to make a student take an honest account of his stock of ideas, throw out the dead matter, place revised price marks on what is left, and try to fill his empty shelves with new goods."

Hostile Learning Environment

Some contemporary critics of academic freedom have embraced the concept of a "hostile learning environment." The concept has been used to support speech codes that suppress expression deemed offensive. That is problematic enough, as we shall see in chapter 7, but it has also been extended to the classroom. On the one hand, some students, concerned with minority rights and gender equality, have expressed concern over the expression of ideas, illustrations, even individual words in class that create discomfort, sometimes demanding that these be preceded by required "trigger warnings"—advance notice that assigned material may contain something that could trigger difficult emotional responses—or even banned. On the other hand, some conservative students charge that the alleged liberal bias of the faculty has led to suppression in the classroom of religious sentiments, including opposition to abortion and gay marriage, or of political views largely disfavored in the academy, including opposition to immigrant rights or to the Black Lives Matter movement. Some have gone so far as to suggest that liberal instructors grade conservative students more harshly, although studies repeatedly show this to be false.[5]

Charges that liberal indoctrination and lack of balance in the classroom create a hostile environment for conservative students have even led to harassment of faculty members and at least one blacklist. The group Turning Point, USA, created a well-funded Professor Watchlist, which purports to identify faculty members who "discriminate against conservative students and advance leftist propaganda in the classroom." It lists names of professors, with their institutional affiliations and photographs, thereby facilitating online stalking and threats. In March 2020, as college instruction moved online in response to the COVID-19 pandemic, the group's founder called on students to submit videos and screen shots from online presentations, declaring that "now is the time to document and expose the radicalism that has been infecting our schools." This was too much for some conservatives. The Charles Koch Foundation, for example, declared that "inciting harassment against scholars isn't just wrong at a time when many are seeking out new ways to engage their students during a crisis, it's always wrong."[6]

For an instructor to engage in discriminatory practices against a student owing to that student's race, ethnicity, gender, sexual orientation, disability, political opinions, or affiliations is, to be sure, an egregious violation of professional ethics—and in some cases may be illegal—and cannot be protected by academic freedom. The academic profession does not have an enforceable code of ethics, as do some other professions, but the AAUP's nonbinding *Statement on Professional Ethics* declares unequivocally that teachers must "avoid any exploitation, harassment, or discriminatory treatment of students."[7] The 1967 *Joint Statement on Rights and Freedoms of Students* adds that professors "should encourage free discussion, inquiry, and expression. Student performance should be evaluated solely on an academic basis, not on opinions or conduct in matters unrelated to academic standards." It is thus improper, *Freedom in the Classroom* reiterates, for any instructor "to hold a student up to obloquy or ridicule in class for advancing an idea grounded in religion . . . politics, or anything else."

In one of the most highly publicized academic freedom cases in recent years, that of Steven Salaita at the University of Illinois (to be discussed in chapter 4), the university's chancellor declared, "What we cannot and will not tolerate at the University of Illinois are personal and disrespectful words or actions that demean and abuse either viewpoints themselves or those who express them." It would, however, be impossible for any university even to function if "viewpoints themselves" could not be subject to critique. "It is neither harassment nor discriminatory treatment of a student to hold up to close criticism an idea or viewpoint the student has posited or advanced," *Freedom in the Classroom* asserted. "Ideas that are germane to a subject under discussion in a classroom cannot be censored because a student with particular religious or political beliefs might be offended. Instruction cannot proceed in the atmosphere of fear that would be produced were a teacher to become subject to administrative sanction based upon the idiosyncratic reaction of one or more students."

In a 2014 statement *On Trigger Warnings*, AAUP's Committee A declared, "The presumption that students need to be protected rather than challenged in a classroom is at once infantilizing and anti-intellectual. It makes comfort a higher priority than intellectual engagement." Demands that students be forewarned about purportedly harmful material ends up, the statement argued, disproportionately affecting politically or socially controversial material, which is "likely to be marginalized if not avoided altogether by faculty who fear complaints for offending or discomforting some of their students." The statement acknowledged that "there may be instances in which a teacher judges it necessary to alert students to potentially difficult material and that is his or her right. Administrative requirements are different from individual faculty decisions. Administration regulation constitutes interference with academic freedom; faculty judgment is a legitimate exercise of autonomy." The statement concluded that "some discomfort is inevitable in classrooms if the goal is to expose students to new ideas, have them question beliefs they have taken for granted, grapple with ethical problems they have never considered, and, more generally, expand their horizons so as to become informed and responsible democratic citizens."

Concern for alleged student discomfort has extended even to charges that professors may engage in sexual harassment when they merely discuss issues of sexuality or use salty language. The AAUP has repeatedly recognized sexual harassment to be a significant problem in higher education and has recommended appropriate policies to address it. However, these policies should not be—but unfortunately far too frequently are—crafted and implemented based on "an overly expansive definition of what amounts and kinds of speech create a 'hostile environment,'" leading to violations of academic freedom through punishment of protected classroom speech.[8]

At the University of Colorado–Boulder, sociology professor Patricia Adler had for years used student assistants to impersonate various kinds of sex workers in a large and highly popular lecture class, "Deviance in US Society," without a problem. Then, in 2013, representatives of the university's Office of Discrimination and Harassment showed up at her class unannounced, although no student had filed a formal complaint about the class. Nevertheless, Adler was accused of sexual harassment and asked to accept a buyout and retire or risk costly disciplinary penalties, including the loss of her retirement benefits. When word got out, her students and many colleagues mobilized in Adler's defense. After the AAUP and other national disciplinary groups also weighed in, the administration backed down. Adler decided to return for a final semester, to teach the course once more before retiring. That semester, she recalled, was "awful." The school's "legal counsel told my colleagues not to talk to me for fear of a lawsuit. . . . I got stalking and scary emails from creepy people. . . . I felt afraid to make a joke in my classroom. . . . I tried as hard as I could to keep the skit," but "the chilling effects . . . made it impossible and I ended up dropping it at the last minute."[9]

At Louisiana State University an education professor was dismissed from her tenured position against the unanimous recommendation of the faculty committee that heard her case. In response, the Faculty Senate by a 39-5 margin voted to censure the administration for this action. The professor was found guilty of sexual harassment based solely on her occasional use of profanity and sexually explicit language with her students. In a report, the AAUP took the LSU administration to task for gross procedural violations in the case, in particular, the completion of a Human Resources investigation that recommended removal before the convening of the faculty committee required by LSU's own rules. The report also expressed concern over LSU administrators' "astonishingly low" tolerance for purportedly offensive language. It pointed out that "as a legal matter isolated off-color comments not directed at anybody in particular do not constitute a hostile work environment or any other violation of sex-discrimination law."[10]

The professor filed a lawsuit for wrongful termination on First Amendment grounds, but the district court and the US Court of Appeals for the Fifth Circuit ruled against her. To gain First Amendment protection, the appellate court determined, classroom speech must involve a "matter of public concern," but "in the college classroom context, speech that does not serve an academic purpose is not of public concern." The professor's remarks, they found, were not relevant to her subject matter. The AAUP's amicus brief in the case emphasized that instructors must be able to employ controversial language to challenge students. "Many things a professor says to his or her students may 'offend' or even 'intimidate' some among them," the brief argued. "If every such statement could lead to formal sanctions, and possibly even loss of employment, the pursuit of knowledge and the testing of ideas in the college classroom would be profoundly chilled."

Academic freedom depends on the protection of diverse voices, including in the classroom. Hence, efforts by colleges and universities to become more diverse, more reflective of the larger community, by attracting students, faculty, and staff from groups historically excluded or underrepresented—efforts that are still far from adequate—are not inconsistent with upholding principles of academic freedom. It is easy to support academic freedom when everyone is saying pretty much the same things. But diverse communities give voice to diverse experiences, diverse assumptions, and diverse needs. And with diversity come disagreement and contention. A more diverse student body and a more diverse faculty will inevitably pose questions for consideration in class that might not have been raised in more homogeneous settings. This is all for the good. At the same time, insults, slurs, demeaning language, or insensitive comments that might previously have gone unchallenged must now be addressed with care and compassion, as must higher education's own historical implication in American systemic racism.

Take, for instance, arguments that some have offered about use in class of the N-word. No one in higher education should tolerate an instructor who employed the word as an insult, but can it even be mentioned or read aloud from a literary or historic text in class? At one university, where an instructor was subject to discipline when the word was repeated from an assigned text by James Baldwin, a faculty group argued that "academic freedom in defense of language that harms students turns the very principle that makes true learning possible into a mechanism for enforcing institutional racism," adding that "further conversations about academic freedom can only take place after we acknowledge that harm has been done to these students." But does mere mention of a loaded term, used by a prominent writer in a classic work, cause "harm?"[11]

In Canada, administrators at one university reacted swiftly to a professor's use of the word in the context of a lecture in which students were asked to reflect on the damaging power of language. The administration declared a blanket ban on all use of the word anywhere, any time, on campus, in any context. That prompted a broad group of Black faculty members and administrators to complain, first, that they had not been consulted on the policy and, second, to explain that the ban would have "a chilling effect on almost anyone who does research relating to blackness, and a seriously harmful effect on the ability of black faculty to teach and speak directly to issues related to blackness, both historically and in the modern world."[12]

Suzanne Nossel, CEO of PEN America, has written that "universities should never punish anyone for merely mentioning a word without any inflection of bigotry." At the same time she sensibly advises that "as stewards of learning professors should be conscious of where a rising generation draws its red lines." Moreover, "individual instructors need not turn their backs on academic freedom to reappraise the pedagogical value of speaking the word in full amid the risk that it will be heard as a slur."[13]

In April 2018, the Faculty Senate at American University approved without dissent a resolution on the relationship between academic freedom and diversity, affirming that "increased attention to issues of diversity, equity, and inclusion need not come at the expense of academic freedom. In fact, a central purpose of academic freedom is precisely to support diversity, equity, and inclusion. The right to dissent—in a civil and respectful manner—must remain sacrosanct in the classroom. . . . Inclusion and academic freedom go hand in hand at institutions of higher learning in free societies aspiring to generate knowledge and wisdom." The very nature of higher education demands contentiousness. Argument and debate, sometimes polarizing, are at the core of the educational enterprise, but neither can thrive without freedom, on the one hand, and the presence of new and challenging perspectives, on the other. Both academic freedom and diversity thus exist to protect and encourage that sort of contention, and should work together to render it constructive.[14]

Controversy and Relevance

The 1940 *Statement* declared that "teachers are entitled to freedom in the classroom in discussing their subject, but they should be careful not to introduce into their teaching controversial matter which has no relation to their subject." This proposes two restrictions on freedom in the classroom. The first, which is obvious, is that academic freedom does not protect instructors who don't teach their subject. An English professor assigned to teach a course on Shakespeare should not transform the class into one on a different writer. But to what extent must this limitation be observed? Should occasional digressions from the subject matter be unprotected or must deviation from assigned curriculum be systematic or in some sense flagrant?

In 1968, on the day after Dr. Martin Luther King Jr. was assassinated, a history professor at the Ohio State University proclaimed at the start of class that he would "suspend the curriculum." He then proceeded to devote the entire session to expounding on the assassination, culminating his lecture by burning his draft card as an expression of his opposition to violence. He was dismissed over faculty objections, and the AAUP investigated. The investigation determined that while dismissal was not warranted, neither were the act of protest and suspension of the curriculum. While a faculty member may be entitled to cancel class on a day of national crisis, or make brief comments on events of the day—indeed, with traumatic events like the King assassination students might find failure to comment heartless—academic freedom does not permit turning a class into a personal protest.[15] On the other hand, it may be appropriate for a faculty member occasionally to devote some class time to pressing current events or university affairs—perhaps a pending strike of campus staff or faculty—or to permit a student group to make some sort of presentation on campus issues not directly related to the course subject.

In 1970, one of the interpretive comments appended to the 1940 *Statement* addressed the second stricture, against introduction of "controversial matter" with "no relation to" the subject. "The intent of this statement is not to discourage what is 'controversial,'" the comment declared. "Controversy is at the heart of the free academic inquiry which the entire statement is designed to foster. The passage serves to underscore the need for teachers to avoid persistently intruding material which has no relation to their subject."

In this light, the 1940 *Statement* must be understood not to limit controversial material but only the *persistent* intrusion of material that is essentially *irrelevant*. But how should that be determined? *Freedom in the Classroom* addressed this question by referring to the AAUP's 1948 investigation of Evansville College in Indiana, where an instructor of religion and philosophy, George Parker, was dismissed for injecting "political discussion" into his classes. Parker was an ardent supporter of the leftist presidential candidacy of Henry Wallace. The investigating committee found no basis for the notion that Parker's frequent digressions into politics were propagandistic. Instead, they argued,

> all experienced teachers realize that it is neither possible nor desirable to exclude rigidly all controversial subjects, or all topics upon which the teacher is not an expert. Many things introduced into the classroom—illustrative material or applications, overtones of significance, illuminating *obiter dicta*—may not be in the bond as far as the subject of the course is concerned, but these and kindred techniques may be of the essence of good teaching. Such techniques are readily distinguishable from calculated, overt "propaganda." . . .
>
> In the nature of the case, judgments concerning the handling of controversial material will frequently depend not so much on the *what* as the *how*. . . . The total effect of what a teacher says on controversial subjects in the classroom depends a great deal upon the manner, the spirit in which he says it and the emphasis he places upon it. It depends also upon the previous existence of a relationship of confidence and understanding between the teacher and his students.[16]

The potential chilling effect of conflicts over controversial classroom teaching was highlighted by a Fall 2020 incident at the University of Southern California Marshall School of Business. A professor was peremptorily removed from teaching a class after he illustrated a point by using a Chinese phrase that could sound similar to the English N-word, but means something entirely different. The school's Faculty Council surveyed the instructional staff for reactions to the move, eliciting repeated concerns about lack of due process but also numerous statements to the effect that the incident would make them more careful, even fearful in class. "I will be more cautious about adding to my course any timely issues in the real world and guiding students' critical thinking," one professor said. "My teaching will be very boring," added another. Yet another expressed regret that the case "will stifle dialogue with my students." The Council concluded from the many responses that while the school's "faculty support[s] efforts to bring greater diversity and inclusion into our classrooms . . . a large proportion . . . think it is too risky for them to continue discussing certain topics with students" because "the current atmosphere is counterproductive both to diversity efforts and to our mission as educators."[17]

Finkin and Post have proposed the following criterion for determining the relation of classroom material to a course's subject: "A pedagogical intervention bears a 'relation' to a subject under consideration if it is educationally relevant. A pedagogical intervention is educationally relevant if it assists students in better understanding a subject under consideration, either in the sense of acquiring greater cognitive mastery of that subject or in the sense of acquiring a more mature apprehension of the import of that subject, which is to say, an improved ability to experience and appreciate the significance of that subject."[18]

"At root, complaints about the persistent interjection of 'irrelevant' material concern the interjection of 'controversial' material," *Freedom in the Classroom* concluded. "The complaints are thus a variant of the charge that instructors have created a 'hostile learning environment' and must be rejected for the reasons we have already discussed. So long as an instructor's allusions provoke genuine debate and learning that is germane to the subject matter of a course, they are protected by 'freedom in the classroom.'"

The Freedom to Teach

In courses for which faculty members are individually responsible, academic freedom in the classroom protects an instructor's right to select the materials to be used; to determine the approach to the subject and the pedagogical methods to be employed; to design the assignments; and to assess student academic performance and record grades—all without having their decisions subject to the veto of a department chair, dean, or other administrative officer. "Academic freedom gives near-absolute power to the professor not because the professor is always right, but because the alternatives are much worse," writes John K. Wilson. "We could have trustees and the government approve all syllabi and provide the 'best' script for professors to recite in the classroom, and the result would be a terrible education."[19]

However, the academic freedom of individual faculty members may be limited by the collective responsibility of the faculty for the institution's curriculum. In many departments, faculty coordinate courses and must come to agreements about course content, syllabi, textbooks, and examinations. Decisions of a faculty body may prevail over the dissenting position of a particular individual member of the faculty, but deliberations leading to such decisions should involve substantial reflection and discussion by all who teach the courses under review. Departments should have a process for periodically reviewing curricular decisions and altering them based on a consensus of the appropriate teaching faculty. Nonetheless, even in such instances, individuals should be able to assign supplementary materials to deal with subjects that they believe are inadequately treated in a required textbook. Instructors also have the right to discuss in the classroom what they see as deficiencies in an assigned textbook. These principles should apply equally to instructors in the tenure system and those with contingent appointments.[20]

Does academic freedom protect the right of a professor to assign his or her own work? The AAUP's Committee on Ethics considered this question in 2004 and concluded that "the right of individual professors to select their own instructional materials, a right protected under principles of academic freedom, should be limited only by such considerations as quality, cost, availability, and the need for coordination with other instructors or courses. Professors should assign readings that best meet the instructional goals of their courses, and they may well conclude that what they themselves have written on a subject best realizes that purpose." The committee recognized, however, that, even though popular notions that professors get rich by assigning their own texts are largely absurd, faculty members may sometimes have a meaningful financial stake in such assignments. Reviewing policies adopted by several universities, the committee endorsed measures designed "to ensure that course-assignment decisions are not compromised by even the appearance of impropriety."

But what if a faculty member or department imposes on *all* those teaching a course a textbook in which one or more colleagues has a financial stake? That question arose at California State University, Fullerton, in 2014. A mathematics professor who refused to use a common textbook was reprimanded and threatened with dismissal. The departmentally designated textbook, a hundred dollars more in cost than the one selected by the professor, was co-authored by the department's chair and vice-chair. There had been no recent review of its use by those assigned to teach the class. "The fact that the book was cheaper was nice," the professor said of his own choice, "but the most important thing, the reason I wanted to teach it, is that it was a better book." A faculty grievance committee acknowledged that the professor had violated department policy, but seemed more concerned that "lack of a policy or mechanism for considering textbook change, coupled with the fact that the department leadership authored the text, created a situation wherein making a change was likely quite difficult." Nonetheless, the university president let the reprimand stand.[21]

In 1997, AAUP's Committee A approved a statement on *The Assignment of Course Grades and Student Appeals*. It concluded, "The assessment of student academic performance . . . including the assignment of particular grades, is a faculty responsibility. Recognizing the authority of the instructor of record to evaluate the academic performance of students enrolled in a course he or she is teaching is a direct corollary of the instructor's 'freedom in the classroom'" ensured by the 1940 *Statement*. It also recognized that a "suitable mechanism for appeal, one which respects both the prerogatives of instructors and the rights of students in this regard" should be available, and offered procedural recommendations.

The AAUP has more than a few times had occasion to call out violations of this policy. In 2004, Benedict College in South Carolina—already on the AAUP's censure list—dismissed three professors for failing to grade students in their courses in accordance with a policy promulgated by the college president. The complicated policy—which had not been reviewed, much less approved, by any faculty body—sought to address an allegedly "excessive" number of poor grades, purportedly leading to large numbers of student withdrawals, by requiring that grades be based as much or more on "effort" as "knowledge" of course material. In 2007, Nicholls State University in Louisiana terminated a mathematics instructor, one day prior to the expiration of her twelfth consecutive annual appointment as a full-time faculty member. The administration offered no rationale, but the most compelling explanation for the move was that failure rates in her classes were higher than expected by an administration concerned that too many students were failing courses. The AAUP investigating committee drew a distinction between this case and the one at Benedict College. "At Benedict the professors chose to disregard what to them was an intrusive and ill-advised official administrative policy," the committee wrote, "while at Nicholls there was no stated policy on grading percentages in college algebra, and [the instructor] was not accused of anything. If the Nicholls administrators perceived a serious problem with the strict grading by a senior instructor, one might have expected them to talk with her about it and see whether an accommodation could be reached."[22]

A third example is perhaps the most egregious. A biologist at Louisiana State University was, according to an AAUP investigating committee, "repeatedly commended for teaching excellence, praised particularly for her 'rigorous approach' and 'demanding coursework'" in upper-division classes. "In spring 2010, in order to 'pitch in,' [she] took on a section of an introductory course for the first time in fifteen years. The grades she assigned for the first test struck the course's coordinator as too low, and he suggested more leniency. Her mid-term grades, however, were more strongly skewed to grades of D and F. The matter was referred to the college dean, who, without consulting her, relieved the instructor from teaching the course." The committee concluded that the LSU administration had violated the faculty's right to assign student grades and, in peremptorily removing a teacher from a course in process, violated her academic freedom to teach.[23]

The greatly expanded use in academic personnel decisions of student evaluations of teaching also poses potential perils for academic freedom. In 1975, the AAUP issued a *Statement on Teaching Evaluation,* which declared that "the emphasis in evaluation should be upon obtaining first-hand evidence of teaching competence, which is most likely to be found among the faculty of a department or college and the students who receive instruction. Evaluation of teaching in which an administrator's judgment is the sole or determining factor is contrary to policies set forth in the *Statement on Government of Colleges and Universities.*" That position was reaffirmed thirty years later in *Observations on the Association's 1975 Statement on Teaching Evaluation.*[24]

Over the past forty years, however, much research has confirmed that reliance on student evaluations—especially if these are reduced to numerical ratings or if individual comments are cherry-picked—should be abandoned because these instruments "do not measure teaching effectiveness" and are greatly influenced by gender and racial biases. They may also be weaponized against faculty in ways that undermine academic freedom. For example, at Barnard College in New York a long-time part-time writing instructor and union activist, whom the administration had previously tried to remove as an unwelcome gadfly, was eventually dismissed on the strength of just two negative student comments on teaching evaluations. As one victim of such weaponization put it, both administrators and unprincipled senior faculty members may "undermine academic freedom through coercing and threatening their untenured and contingent colleagues to conform to a narrow set of norms around teaching, scholarship, 'standards,' and academic hierarchy that they have decided to police."[25]

A similar development with problematic implications for academic freedom has been the movement for mandated assessment of student "learning outcomes" at the level of the individual class, the degree program, and the institution as a whole. These programs are often mandated by state education agencies or federally recognized accrediting agencies and aggressively imposed on faculties by administrators, at times with near-evangelical zeal. Frequently they mimic industrial management techniques and privilege quantitative measurements, reflecting the anti-intellectual conviction that "any alleged knowledge which can be expressed in figures is in fact as final and exact as the figures in which it is expressed."[26] Whether these mechanisms, which may vary quite radically, are meant to provide a diagnostic tool for self-improvement or furnish a basis for budgetary allocations and even evaluation of faculty is often unclear, although there is good reason to fear that the latter motivations have been paramount.

While it seems logical that those who pay for education have a right to learn the extent to which their investment has been productive, it is also worth noting, as the AAUP did in a 1991 report, *Mandated Assessment of Educational Outcomes,* that "undergraduates in American postsecondary education, and their academic programs, are more intensively and perhaps more frequently evaluated than are those in postsecondary education anywhere else in the world." With respect to academic freedom, advocates of assessment programs deny they will undercut the faculty's authority over curriculum, both in individual classes and more generally. Experience, however, suggests otherwise, as more and more teachers complain that assessment regimes restrict their choices of pedagogies, create burdensome paperwork, and devalue their professional judgment.

While voicing skepticism about the necessity and effectiveness of mandated assessment programs, the 1991 AAUP report acknowledged that "agencies charged with the oversight of higher education, and the larger public and the diverse constituencies that colleges and universities represent, have a legitimate stake in the effectiveness of teaching and learning. Their insistence that colleges and universities provide documented evidence of effectiveness is appropriate." However, "the justification for developing any assessment plan in a given case, whether voiced by a legislative body, the governing board, or one or more administrative officers, must be accompanied by a clear showing that existing methods of assessing learning are inadequate for accomplishing the intended purposes of a supplementary plan, and that the mandated procedures are consistent with effective performance of the institutional mission." The report enumerated a series of standards that all mandated assessment programs should meet. Two are of critical importance: (1) "The faculty should have primary responsibility for establishing the criteria for assessment and the methods for implementing it." (2) "Externally mandated assessment procedures are not appropriate for the evaluation of individual students or faculty members and should not be used for that purpose." Should these precepts be violated, any mandated assessment program will no longer only endanger academic freedom in teaching—it will violate it.[27]

The Electronic Classroom

Since 2004, the AAUP has held that "academic freedom, free inquiry, and freedom of expression within the academic community may be limited to no greater extent in electronic format than they are in print." As more teaching moves into online and other remote formats, "the concept of 'classroom' must be broadened," the AAUP stressed in its 2013 policy *Academic Freedom and Electronic Communications,* "to reflect how instruction increasingly occurs through a medium that clearly has no physical boundaries."[28]

In addition to those challenges that online classes share with sessions held in a physical space, online teaching can present new difficulties for academic freedom in teaching. In 1999, the AAUP noted that "teachers should have the same responsibility for selecting and presenting materials in courses offered through distance-education technologies as they have in those offered in traditional classroom settings." However, as historian of technology David Noble noted, "once faculty and courses go online, administrators gain much greater control over faculty performance and course content." The AAUP has pointed out how "new teaching technologies also allow faculty members and students to be monitored in new ways." For example, a state politician seeking to discipline a University of Mississippi professor subpoenaed all materials uploaded to the instructor's Blackboard account as well as all communications sent or received via that account.[29]

The widespread use of remote learning via commercial platforms such as Zoom, which accompanied higher education's response to the COVID-19 pandemic, has raised questions about how much power such platforms should have. At San Francisco State University, a campus roundtable discussion with a highly controversial speaker, previously guilty of terrorism, was scheduled to be hosted on Zoom, but under pressure from outside groups the company refused to host the discussion. Efforts to stream the session on Facebook and YouTube were also rejected. While the incident was isolated, it revealed the potential for conflict between academic values and commercial interests. Concerns have also been raised about the employment by Zoom and similar providers of servers in China, where state surveillance of the internet is common, which may endanger Chinese students studying at US institutions. Questions have been raised as well about campus policies mandating use of online learning management systems like Blackboard, which may constrain faculty freedom to teach.[30]

According to the 1915 *Declaration*, the "classroom utterances of college and university teachers . . . ought always to be considered privileged communications. Discussions in the classroom ought not to be supposed to be utterances for the public at large. They are often designed to provoke opposition or arouse debate." Today incidents in which students have surreptitiously recorded remarks by professors, or even by fellow students, and then shared the recordings widely via social media, sometimes in tendentiously edited or even doctored form, has called new attention to this principle. Some have wondered why such recordings differ from a student who takes careful notes and disseminates them. But recordings may be abused in ways that would be more difficult with notes. To be sure, there are legitimate justifications for permitting some students to record classes—as an accommodation to disability, for example. And the expansion of online instruction during the pandemic has created new arguments for recording classes and making them available to students who may have limited access to the internet. Nonetheless, the potential for abuse of recordings by both those enrolled in a class and those facilitating its transmission remains.

Even before the advent of the internet, groups like today's Professor Watchlist sought to expose the alleged bias of the faculty. They encouraged recording of classroom statements for purported accuracy. In 1985, the AAUP and twelve other higher education organizations jointly responded, declaring "the presence in the classroom of monitors for an outside organization will have a chilling effect on the academic freedom of both students and faculty members." That principle holds true whether the classroom is physical or virtual.

The spread of online education has also raised issues of faculty intellectual property in teaching materials. The AAUP's 2013 *Statement on Intellectual Property* declared:

> Course syllabi at many institutions are considered public documents; indeed, they may be posted on universally accessible websites. It is thus to be expected that teachers everywhere will learn from one another's syllabi and that syllabi will be disseminated as part of the free exchange of academic knowledge. Faculty lectures or original audiovisual materials, however, unless specifically and voluntarily created as works made for hire, constitute faculty intellectual property. As components of faculty-designed online courses, they cannot be revised, edited, supplemented, or incorporated into courses taught by others without the consent of the original creator. Nor can an online course as a whole be assigned to another instructor without the consent of the faculty member who created the course, unless, once again, the faculty member agreed to treat the course as a work made for hire with such ownership rights residing in the institution. Faculty governing bodies have a special—and increasing—responsibility to ensure that faculty members are not pressured to sign work-for-hire agreements against their will.[31]

The Limitations Clause

"If a church or religious denomination establishes a college to be governed by a board of trustees, with the express understanding that the college will be used as an instrument of propaganda in the interests of the religious faith professed by the church or denomination creating it," the 1915 *Declaration* declared, "the trustees have a right to demand that everything be subordinated to that end." Such institutions, however, were already "rare and becoming ever more rare." Insofar as they still existed, like secular "proprietary" institutions, they "should not be permitted to sail under false colors."

The 1940 *Statement*'s definition of academic freedom in teaching included this sentence: "Limitations of academic freedom because of religious or other aims of the institution should be clearly stated in writing at the time of the appointment." The sentence has become known as the limitations clause. The authors of the 1970 interpretive comments added to that clause this explanatory note: "Most church-related institutions no longer need or desire the departure from the principle of academic freedom implied in the 1940 *Statement*, and we do not now endorse such a departure."

The comment came partly in response to the 1967 Land-of-Lakes Statement by a group of Catholic university presidents, led by Rev. Theodore Hesburgh of Notre Dame, which declared that their institutions could not thrive without autonomy and academic freedom. At the same time, many evangelical institutions had managed to weaken the hold of fundamentalism on their teachings. Nonetheless, fifty years later the comment seems unduly optimistic. It is not only that more than a handful of religiously based institutions still delineate limitations on academic freedom in faculty contracts. More worrisome is that many others frequently seek to impose such limitations arbitrarily or to apply them overbroadly. Although the 1970 comment did not read the clause out of the *Statement*, the AAUP would still come to consider that religious institutions that "gain, or seek, broader recognition as seats of higher learning—e.g., by expanding their curricula, by identifying themselves as universities or colleges of liberal education, by awarding secular degrees, by securing regional or specialized accreditation, and by appealing to the public for support on those grounds"—should be fully subject to the provisions of the 1940 *Statement*.[32]

The most noteworthy such case investigated by the AAUP was that of Professor Charles Curran at the Catholic University of America in 1988. The case had its origins in 1967, when Professor Curran, a liberal theologian, was unanimously recommended for reappointment and promotion by the School of

Theology and the Academic Senate. The Board of Trustees, at the time composed mostly of bishops, rejected the recommendation. In what the 1989 AAUP investigation would call "a landmark in the history of American higher education," the university's faculty voted 400-18 to launch a strike in protest, which was soon joined by large numbers of students. After five days, the administration backed down.

Curran, however, remained a target of continuing and intensifying criticism from the Vatican—unlike other American Catholic schools, Catholic University is responsible directly to Rome—and in 1986 he was informed that he could "no longer exercise the function of a Professor of Catholic Theology at the Catholic University of America." Curran was afforded a hearing by an ad hoc committee of the Academic Senate, but the university withdrew his "canonical mission" and sought to reassign him to a position in ethics and sociology. The AAUP's investigation determined that Curran lost his theology position "because of opinions expressed in his published works." The investigating committee concluded that the limitations clause did not apply, first, because "Catholic University has no statement labeled 'limitations,'" and policies that might have suggested such limits were not applicable to the case. Second, the committee noted that the university had reported to its accrediting agency agreement with the statement that a "university conceived as a community of scholars must be free of arbitrary and extrinsic constraints, be they civil or ecclesiastical. Institutional autonomy and academic freedom are essential conditions of university life and growth." Curran declined the reassignment and left the university.[33]

In 2016, Wheaton College in Illinois initiated termination proceedings against a tenured professor of political science who wore a hijab as a gesture of solidarity with Muslims. The evangelical Protestant college said it objected to the way she described her action on her Facebook page, specifically her claim that Christians and Muslims worship the "same God." Wheaton claimed the professor had violated its Statement of Faith. Such a statement might, consistent with the limitations clause, exempt Wheaton from AAUP investigation and censure given that, by requiring new faculty to sign the statement, the college had "disclose[d] its restrictions on academic freedom to prospective members of the faculty." Many academic organizations and individuals saw the college's move as a violation of academic freedom nonetheless, several noting that there was nothing in the statement of faith, which consists of twelve core religious beliefs, that had obviously been violated. Emails from the college provost also suggested that public image was of more concern than theology. Wheaton initiated a review process in the case that included convening a faculty committee to determine whether or to what extent the faith statement had been violated, but before the process could be completed the professor negotiated a settlement with the school and departed voluntarily.[34]

The place of academic freedom at religiously based institutions, be they Catholic, Protestant, Jewish, or Islamic, remains a subject of at times heated contention. But today the focus is shifting from attempts to control theological instruction toward efforts to teach political viewpoints as if they were religious ones. Here the premier example of what the historian Richard Hofstadter called "secularized fundamentalism" is Liberty University, led by Jerry Falwell Jr. until his departure in 2020, amid a sex and financial scandal.[35] Liberty has no tenure system. Its faculty handbook declares that "all employees of the University are expected to conduct themselves in matters of language and morality in a manner compatible with the Mission of the University and The Liberty Way. Unsuitable conduct may be grounds for disciplinary action, up to and including termination." On its website, Liberty proclaims that "all of our courses are taught from a Christian perspective and our faculty sees themselves as mentors. Our mission is to Train Champions for Christ." Yet Liberty offers a broad array of degree programs in subject areas distant from religion, including law, medicine, nursing, and epidemiology. The notion that these should be exempt from the protections of academic freedom on the basis of the limitations clause is absurd. The policies of institutions like Liberty, one journalist charged, "have serious political implications."[36] They have serious consequences as well for faculty members' exercise of their academic freedom not only in their teaching but in their expression as citizens, discussed in the next chapter.

Chapter 4

Citizenship

The 1915 *Declaration*'s inclusion of protection for "extramural utterances," reaffirmed in the 1940 *Statement*'s claim that "when they speak and write as citizens" faculty members "should be free from institutional censorship or discipline," has been called "the most distinctively American contribution to the theory of academic freedom" and its "most theoretically problematic aspect."[1]

It is also the element of academic freedom most closely resembling classic principles of freedom of speech and hence is often confused with that right. In 1930, the philosopher Arthur Lovejoy, an author of the 1915 *Declaration*, wrote that while disciplinary actions against those exercising "their ordinary political or personal freedom" may offend the "spirit of academic freedom," they are "primarily a special case of the abuse of the economic relation of employer and employee for the denial of civil liberties." More recently, David Bromwich has conceived of academic freedom as "a category of political freedom," which "belongs to the larger class of rights enjoyed by citizens of a free society." Judith Butler distinguishes academic freedom from the right to political expression. The two, however, "converge when academics who speak 'extramurally' suffer retaliation or punishment." Legal scholars Erwin Chemerinsky and Howard Gilman divide a "professional zone" of teaching and research protected by academic freedom from a "free speech zone" protected by free speech principles.[2]

Justifying a defense of extramural expression on free speech grounds instead of on grounds of academic freedom will often make little practical difference, especially at a public university, where the First Amendment applies, but the distinction remains crucial. Welcome as it surely would be if stronger protections for free expression extended to a wider range of employment relationships, US citizens are entitled by law to free speech protection only against government sanctions, not those of private employers. Unless an employment contract provides safeguards, the weight of the "at-will" principle in US employment law provides little legal recourse for the great majority of private employees, who enjoy almost no security from employer sanction for expression off the job. Even where government is the employer, such protections may be limited.

The rationale supporting free speech also differs from that for academic freedom. The former assumes that all individuals have a democratic and egalitarian civil right to speak their minds, largely without consideration of any limit other than their own consciences and without regard to how informed on a topic they may be. Professors are held to a different standard in the classroom and in their scholarship, where, as we've seen, their expressive rights are based on and limited by their training and expertise. Hence, one might ask, if professors speak publicly on matters outside their area of competence, or violate disciplinary standards in public expression related to their expertise, why should colleges and universities protect that speech beyond what the law may require? How can protecting extramural expression be justified as an element of academic freedom?

A Prophylactic Approach

Finkin and Post argue that academic freedom for extramural expression can best be justified if it is viewed as "a prophylactic protection for freedom of research and teaching."[3] The origins of this position may be found in an early debate between John Henry Wigmore, dean of the Northwestern University Law School and the AAUP's second president, and Lovejoy. Wigmore compared academic freedom to judicial immunity. A judge cannot be held liable "for a wrong done by him while acting on matters within his jurisdiction and as a judge," he argued; therefore, a professor should be immune from discipline "so long as he keeps within his own jurisdiction." However, he emphasized, "the scholar must not expect protection if he goes outside of the field to which he is appointed."

In this formulation, protection for extramural expression becomes essentially an application of the protection offered for research. Lovejoy disagreed. On the one hand, he thought it wrong to fully shield professors for public comments even in their discipline, since that would protect them if the comments were, judged by disciplinary standards, "incompetent." On the other hand, protecting public expression only in a professor's area of competence would "make it possible for trustees who wished to eliminate from an institution an economist of whose economic theories they disapproved, to dismiss him because of an allegation of disagreement between their views and his own on political science or on the theory of evolution." Lovejoy concluded, "in order effectively to protect the investigator *within* his special province, you must protect him outside of it also."[4]

Princeton political scientist Keith Whittington has summarized the argument well. He stresses that "if faculty members could be dismissed for what they say in public then the core mission of the university to advance and disseminate knowledge would come under pressure and be subverted." Because scholars "are properly subject to discipline if their teaching and research do not meet professional standards, on first impression we might think it would be unobjectionable if scholars were held to the same standards when they speak publicly about issues that fall within their expertise. But professors are likely to fall short of our normal expectations for scholarly discourse when engaging in public debate." Moreover, attenuating Lovejoy's concern about incompetence, he continues,

> if professors are being drawn into public debates about matters relating to their research, then that would suggest that their research is necessarily going to be seen as controversial. Pressuring colleges and universities to sanction those professors because of the controversial content of their extramural speech would be tantamount to pressuring them to sanction professors for the controversial content of their scholarly research. If extramural speech were unprotected, faculty members could secure a refuge for pursuing their scholarship about controversial topics unmolested only if they assiduously refrained from bringing that scholarship to public attention.

With respect to expression on topics remote from a scholar's disciplinary expertise, Whittington echoes Lovejoy, noting that failure to protect such speech

> would leave professors vulnerable to being dismissed from their positions for pretextual reasons. . . . Extramural speech would become a loophole by which administrators could circumvent tenure and gut academic freedom. . . . [Professors] would appropriately be less willing to say what they think is true and embark on new paths of discovery if they worried that an unguarded public remark that generated controversy could become the basis for dismissal. . . . A faculty intent on self-censorship to avoid the possibility of becoming a source of public controversy is unlikely to be able to pursue research confidently or facilitate lively classroom discussions. . . . We should be concerned with protecting the ability of the biology professor to express ill-informed

opinions about politics . . . because the kind of stultifying intellectual environment in which one is wary of expressing a political opinion is not likely to be conducive to the voicing of bold new ideas and the rigorous exploration of them.[5]

The Fitness Standard

The authors of the 1915 *Declaration* did not believe that professors should "be debarred from giving expression to their judgments upon controversial questions, or that their freedom of speech, outside the university, should be limited to questions falling within their own specialties." Yet, they acknowledged, such freedom is constrained by the academic's "peculiar obligation to avoid hasty or unverified or exaggerated statements, and to refrain from intemperate or sensational modes of expression." A professor's right to freedom of public expression "in no sense . . . implies that individual teachers should be exempt from all restraints as to the matter or manner of their utterances, either within or without the university." However, such restraints "should, in the main, . . . be self-imposed, or enforced by the public opinion of the profession." Moreover, should discipline be called for, it "cannot with safety be taken by bodies not composed of members of the academic profession." The 1940 *Statement* similarly warned that when scholars "speak or write as citizens . . . they should remember that the public may judge their profession and their institution by their utterances. Hence they should at all times be accurate, should exercise appropriate restraint, should show respect for the opinions of others, and should make every effort to indicate that they are not speaking for the institution."

Should infringements of the *Declaration*'s calls to avoid exaggeration and intemperance, or the *Statement*'s "special obligations" to ensure accuracy, restraint, and respect, justify institutional discipline? Or are these to be taken as essentially instructive exhortations to good behavior?

Those questions troubled the negotiations leading to the 1940 *Statement*. In a 1938 draft, the paragraph defining obligations of faculty members engaging in extramural expression concluded with this sentence: "The judgment of what constitutes fulfillment of these obligations should rest with the individual."[6] That would have made obvious the advisory nature of the statement's strictures. But the Association of American Colleges, the AAUP's administration partner in the effort, would not have it, the statement was deleted, and the following "interpretation" was added:

> If the administration of a college or university feels that a teacher has not observed the admonitions of paragraph 3 of the section on Academic Freedom and believes that the extramural utterances of the teacher have been such as to raise grave doubts concerning the teacher's fitness for his or her position, it may proceed to file charges under paragraph 4 of the section on Academic Tenure. In pressing such charges, the administration should remember that teachers are citizens and should be accorded the freedom of citizens. In such cases the administration must assume full responsibility, and the American Association of University Professors and the Association of American Colleges are free to make an investigation.

This interpretation was included only as a note following the text, but it established firmly that "professional fitness" should be the criterion for determining when extramural expression might be subject to institutional discipline. As to who would determine such fitness, the AAUP held that it must be a duly representative and qualified faculty body.

The fitness standard was tested in 1960, when the student newspaper at the University of Illinois printed a letter from an untenured assistant professor of botany, Leo Koch. His letter, responding to an article criticizing campus attitudes toward sex, condoned premarital relations. A local clergyman, himself a former Communist, soon accused the young botanist of following "the standard operating procedure of the Communist conspiracy" in order to "subvert the religious and moral foundations of America." The university president condemned the article as "offensive and repugnant," suspended Koch immediately, and terminated his appointment at the end of the academic year. The faculty senate's academic freedom committee upheld Koch's right to "express views on sexual behavior" and criticized the administration for acting "contrary to the standards of proper procedure in a dismissal case." Nonetheless, the committee also called Koch's letter "a clear violation of academic responsibility" and recommended a reprimand. The recommendation was ignored, however, and Koch was dismissed.

The subsequent AAUP investigation was led by Yale law professor Thomas Emerson, a preeminent civil libertarian. Attempting to apply the admonitions of the 1940 *Statement* and the interpretive note, Emerson concluded that "university sanctions cannot be applied where legal sanctions would not be." The implication was that a faculty member could *never* be disciplined for extramural expression unless that expression fell under one of the few narrow exceptions to the First Amendment upheld by the US Supreme Court. For AAUP's Committee A, that was a bridge too far. In 1963, Emerson's report was published in two parts, the first with findings on due process and the right to make controversial statements with which Committee A agreed, and the second as a separate discussion of "academic responsibility" signed by Emerson's investigating committee alone.[7]

In 1964, Committee A's chair reiterated that "only demonstrated lack of professional fitness for the position can constitute grounds for dismissal."[8] The committee took up the question once more, however, issuing the *Statement on Extramural Utterances*, which has guided AAUP policy ever since. It recognized this "controlling principle":

A faculty member's expression of opinion as a citizen cannot constitute grounds for dismissal unless it clearly demonstrates the faculty member's unfitness to serve. Extramural utterances rarely bear upon the faculty member's fitness for continuing service. Moreover, a final decision should take into account the faculty member's entire record as a teacher and scholar. In the absence of weighty evidence of unfitness, the administration should not prefer charges; and if it is not clearly proved in the hearing that the faculty member is unfit to continue, the faculty committee should make a finding in favor of the faculty member concerned.[9]

When, in 1970, the AAUP and the AAC negotiated interpretive comments to be inserted into the 1940 *Statement*, one comment explicitly incorporated this "controlling principle" language from the 1964 *Statement*. The AAUP still holds to this principle and considers the 1940 "special obligations" as largely hortatory.

On what grounds might a faculty member be considered unfit to teach? The AAUP committee that in 1956 investigated violations of academic freedom during the anti-Communist purges included "incompetence, lack of scholarly objectivity or integrity, serious misuse of the classroom or of academic prestige, [and] gross personal misconduct" among potential grounds, if "established by evidence." But the committee also recognized that "an unpopular exercise of the rights of free speech and petition, even when it brings about adverse publicity, does not in and of itself justify" disciplinary action. "Of itself it raises no question about a professor's fitness."[10]

In 1971, the AAUP investigated the dismissal of Angela Davis, a declared Communist, from a temporary position in the philosophy department at UCLA by the University of California Board of Regents, which had overruled decisions by campus faculty and administrators. Although the regents were plainly motivated by hostility to Davis's political affiliation, they ostensibly based their decision on four speeches she delivered that allegedly violated the admonitions of the 1940 *Statement*. In its report the investigating committee further elaborated the meaning of the fitness standard. "What is required by the concept 'fitness for one's position?'" they asked.

Most obviously, it means the capability and the willingness to carry out the duties of the position. . . . To meet the AAUP's standard of unfitness, then, the faculty member's shortcoming must be shown to bear some identified relation to his capacity or willingness to perform the responsibilities, broadly conceived, to his students, to his colleagues, to his discipline, or to the functions of his institution, that pertain to his assignment. Thus, under the quoted principles, institutional sanctions imposed for extramural utterances can be a violation of academic freedom even when the utterances themselves fall short of the standards of the profession; for it is central to that freedom that the faculty member, when speaking as a citizen, "should be free from institutional censorship or discipline" except insofar as his behavior is shown, on the whole record, to be incompatible with fitness for his position.

The report then added:

At some stage in a contested argument over academic responsibility and fitness to teach, appeal must be made to someone's judgment in applying what are necessarily somewhat imprecise standards for the limits of propriety of extramural controversy. The judgment to be made is how far the condemned polemics fall below a professionally tolerable norm, and about the gravity, the frequency, and other circumstances of the incidents along with other evidence bearing on the speaker's overall academic responsibility. It is entirely possible, even likely, that the balance might be struck differently on the same evidence by leaders of the academic community and by members of a governing board, especially where political and other public controversy is involved. . . . In the light of these considerations, the wisdom of the AAUP procedural standards—which require careful exchange of views between faculty committees, administrations, and governing boards in disciplinary actions of the present kind—is apparent.[11]

It is sometimes suggested that when a teacher's extramural expression so deeply offends an ethnic, racial, religious, or other group to the extent that members of that group might feel unwelcome or fear unfair treatment in that instructor's classes, action should be taken. But unless the expression can be shown to affect a professor's "fitness," such action must be strictly limited. Take, for instance, the case of Arthur Butz, an electrical engineering professor at Northwestern University who is also one of the nation's premier Holocaust deniers. As far as anyone can determine, he has never brought up these ideas in his classes, nor is the topic relevant to his research or his ability to teach engineering. But while his views, however repellent, are and should be protected by academic freedom, might not Jewish students enrolled in his classes fear they would be treated unfairly, even if no evidence has emerged to suggest that he has ever been discriminatory? Out of caution, Northwestern enacted a policy whereby if Butz ever teaches a course required for graduation, a different section with a different instructor will also be offered. Of course, were Butz a professor of modern European history, his Holocaust denial could ipso facto disqualify him as a teacher and scholar in that field.[12]

Then there is the case of Amy Wax, a professor at the University of Pennsylvania's School of Law. In 2017, she wrote approvingly that "everyone wants to go to countries ruled by white Europeans" because those are the countries that display "superior" cultural values. Two years later, at the National Conservatism Conference, Wax gave a speech calling for stricter immigration restrictions, arguing that "we are better off if our country is dominated numerically, demographically, politically, at least in fact if not formally, by people from the First World, from the West, than by people from countries that had failed to advance." In an interview she asserted, "I don't think I've ever seen a black student graduate in the top quarter of the [Penn Law School] class and rarely, rarely in the top half." That claim was easily refuted, and Wax was denounced by her dean and her colleagues and barred from teaching mandatory first-year classes.

In a blog post Whittington called this "a classic example of 'extramural speech,'" adding that "there are limits to academic freedom, but Wax's critics have not yet shown she has crossed them." Are Wax's expressed views relevant to her "fitness" to teach a student body that the faculty and administration are striving to diversify? "Professors are allowed to denigrate groups of people in such a way that students might fear that they will not be treated fairly in the classroom," Whittington argued. "Professors are not allowed to in fact treat students unfairly. . . . That students are made uncomfortable by the fact that a professor might think badly of a group to which they belong—or even think badly of an individual student!—does not define the boundary of academic freedom." Moreover, he continued, the argument against Amy Wax is the same argument "that has been turned against professors who engage in racially inflammatory rhetoric that might make white students think they would be judged by the color of their skin."[13]

On the other hand, might it be argued that Wax's repeated disparagement of minorities, including of minority students at Penn, creates a situation in which such students could genuinely expect she would not treat them fairly, even if evidence that she has actually discriminated remains inadequate? And could it therefore not be said that this might be relevant to her fitness to teach? After all, by restricting Wax's teaching assignment to non-required classes her administration already had in effect concluded that her extramural expression was relevant to her fitness for at least one portion of her job. Removal from teaching required classes can be seen as a legitimate use of institutional authority to assign workload. Faculty appointments, including those with tenure, do not guarantee that appointees will be able to teach the classes they desire. On the other hand, there is at least a whiff of disciplinary action in such reassignment. Could it not be interpreted as punishment? That question would best be resolved through academic due process at the institutional level.

It would be—and most definitely should be—extremely difficult to dismiss a tenured faculty member for unfitness on the grounds that her extramural expression alone could create a classroom atmosphere so intimidating to the learning of some students that this implicates her fitness for the position. In principle, however, this is not inconceivable. Still, extreme caution must be exercised. Expanding the notion of fitness to accommodate the concerns of students about what an instructor *might* do based solely on extramural comments, would be highly dangerous, and in such cases accumulating sufficient evidence to demonstrate a prejudicial pattern of behavior could prove a daunting task.

Social Media

When Leo Koch wrote his letter, and Angela Davis addressed protest rallies, their audiences numbered a few thousand at best. Today, however, the internet reaches millions around the globe in seconds. Anyone who posts a controversial statement may unwittingly incite an online mob. Social media may blur the distinction between the private and the public. Posts that are made with the expectation that they will be accessible only to a small group may find an audience of millions. Social media also can preserve random comments, which may be taken from their initial context in ways that exaggerate or distort their meaning. Interest groups may find it useful to stoke outrage by publicizing controversial social media statements. Expression by faculty members in traditional media, including scholarly publications, may be tendentiously excerpted, quoted, or caricatured and then circulated to a vast online readership, often with appeals to let the faculty member's institution know that such expression must be punished. In many cases, professors are subjected to abuse and harassment, including threats to their lives and families.

Much of this activity is the result of work by well-funded organizations and media outlets, but individuals, including students, may raise alarms about a faculty member's posting that can attract a large following. In 2020, a Wisconsin professor posted an ill-considered remark on Facebook concerning sexual harassment; it prompted a student to initiate a petition for her dismissal that gathered more than 100,000 signatures, prompting condemnation, but no disciplinary action, by her university administration.[14]

A significant amount of the harassment has been racially motivated. In 2017, a tenured professor in sociology at Trinity College in Connecticut posted an online response to a police shooting that some charged advocated violence. The post was picked up by a right-wing website that monitors faculty expression, and within hours the professor and his family had received death threats. Two Republican legislators called on Trinity "to immediately, and permanently, remove" the offending professor from the faculty. He was placed on involuntary leave. Only after the campus and national AAUP exerted pressure did Trinity acknowledge that a faculty member's expression as a citizen is protected by academic freedom. In a similar case, an African-American philosophy professor at Texas A&M University was targeted for harassment after a conservative magazine took out of context a four-year-old comment he had made. Instead of defending his academic freedom, the university president publicly declared the comment "disturbing" and "in stark contrast to Aggie core values." The professor has since taken a position at a university abroad.[15]

Extramural expression of a very different sort about race was at issue when, in 2020, the business school at Catholic University in Washington, DC, suspended and then fired an adjunct assistant professor in response to allegedly racist tweets about Barack Obama, Michelle Obama, and Kamala Harris. The tweets, the school's dean wrote, "would be interpreted by a reasonable person to be racist and/or sexist." Faculty members, the dean wrote, are expected to be both "great teachers" and "role models" for students. "Your Twitter activity . . . is inconsistent with being such a role model." In a letter to the university's president, the AAUP noted that the professor's "allegation that the administration's action against him violated his academic freedom of extramural utterance . . . stands unrebutted" in the absence of a due process hearing by a representative faculty body.[16]

As the AAUP first stated in 2004, "Academic freedom, free inquiry, and freedom of expression within the academic community may be limited to no greater extent in electronic format than they are in print."[17] College and university administrations, therefore, must apply to a faculty member's statements on social media the same fitness standard appropriate for older formats. They must also defend faculty members against the proliferation of threats directed against them and staunchly resist threats and ultimatums directed at the institution. Campus safety, while a legitimate consideration, is not a valid excuse for suspending a faculty member targeted by harassers. As the AAUP said in 2017, "Anything short of a vigorous defense of academic freedom will only further imperil safety. Concessions to the harassers send the message that such odious tactics are effective."[18]

In 2013, a professor at the University of Kansas tweeted a comment about gun control that offended gun advocates. The university formally reaffirmed its commitment to academic freedom, but the professor was suspended "to avoid disruption." The incident prompted the state Board of Regents to adopt rules under which faculty members could be suspended or dismissed "for improper use of social media," which the policy defined as "any facility for online publication and commentary," a definition so broad it arguably could include emails and even online periodicals and books. The rules defined "improper use" as including communications "contrary to the best interests of the university" or that impair "discipline by superiors or harmony among co-workers."[19] Such provisions manifestly violate academic freedom.

The most notorious case in recent years of a professor dismissed for extramural expression on social media was that of Professor Steven Salaita at the University of Illinois. Salaita, who is of Palestinian heritage, was hired to a tenured position and was about to begin his new job when the administration and trustees learned of a series of inflammatory comments on Twitter he had made about the Israeli-Palestinian conflict. Because his appointment was still formally subject to trustee approval—a process at the time almost always incomplete when newly hired faculty members arrived—it was withdrawn at the last minute. The move generated immediate controversy and extensive criticism directed at the university, a lawsuit filed by Professor Salaita (subsequently settled with payment of damages), and AAUP censure (since removed).

The administration did not contend that Salaita's remarks demonstrated unfitness in scholarship. Nor did they claim concern about "his positions on the conflict in the Middle East" or "his criticism of Israel." Instead, Chancellor Phyllis Wise argued, "it was the tone of his tweets that lay at the core of the problem." Wise and the university's trustees insisted that the fitness of a scholar and teacher can and even should be judged according to a standard of "civility," which, they implied, should outweigh protections for academic freedom. The trustees claimed that disrespectful speech "is not an acceptable form of civil argument" and "has no place . . . in our democracy."[20]

These appeals to civility were not the only ones issued by higher education leaders at the time. In 2014, Nicholas Dirks, chancellor of the University of California at Berkeley, marked the fiftieth anniversary of that institution's famous Free Speech Movement with a statement proposing that "courteousness and respect in words and deeds are basic preconditions to any meaningful exchange of ideas. In this sense, free speech and civility are two sides of a single coin—the coin of open, democratic society." Few academics do not value civil discourse, which has, if anything, since then further eroded, often to the detriment of academic freedom. However, administrative demands for civility may endanger academic freedom when applied to the extramural expression of faculty members. Responding to both Dirks and the Salaita case, UCLA historian Michael Meranze wrote,

> The demand for civility effectively outlaws a range of intellectual, literary, and political forms: satire is not civil, caricature is not civil, hyperbole and aesthetic mockery are not civil nor is polemic. Ultimately the call for civility is a demand that you not express anger; and if it was enforced it would suggest that there is nothing to be angry about in the world. The call for civility in discourse confuses the enforcement of administrative time, place, and manner restrictions with the genuine need to defend people from personal threat. The result is that the administrative desire trumps all else. . . .
>
> Members of the university community don't need to be told to behave; instead, we need to demand of ourselves that we support our claims with evidence and coherence. We don't need to pretend that all debates are friendly ones or that there are not real interests in conflict. If universities . . . are going to model intellectual discourse and life for the country, it is not going to be by imposing some rule of tone; it is going to be by demanding of people that they argue with reasons.[21]

Absent genuine threats to an individual or individuals, a faculty member's social media postings are never, by themselves, convincing evidence of unfitness and should therefore never be the sole basis for dismissal or severe sanction.

The BDS Movement

For over a decade, one of the more disruptive controversies on some campuses has been that over the boycott, divestment, and sanctions (BDS) movement directed against the state of Israel. The tragic and seemingly intractable conflict between Israel and the Palestinians has engendered impassioned debates and arguments among faculty and students, with the discussion often tarnished by accusations of, on one side, antisemitism and, on the other, Islamophobia. These charges have at times been valid, but often they only forestall dialogue.

The controversy has mostly impacted the free speech rights of students and outside speakers, but at times the faculty's academic freedom has also been imperiled, the Salaita case offering one example. With alarming frequency, advocates on both sides embrace their own academic freedom and freedom of speech while denying it to their opponents. At San Francisco State University a pro-Israel group plastered the campus with posters declaring a Palestinian-American ethnic studies professor and BDS advocate a "terrorist." On the other side, a pro-Israel philosophy professor at Connecticut College was compelled to take two semesters of sabbatical after receiving numerous death threats in response to one of his Facebook posts. As Kenneth Stern, director of the Bard Center for the Study of Hate, has written, "campus partisans on each side of the Israel/Palestine debate repeatedly corrode the academy's core value of academic freedom, as they try to censor and suppress their opponents." He adds, "Pro-Palestinian students might try to censor by shouting, disrupting, and heckling; Jewish organizations tend to work through connections to administrators and donors, with phone calls and emails. But the goal—diminishing the other side's ability to speak—is the same."[22]

The Palestinian Campaign for the Academic and Cultural Boycott of Israel was initiated in 2004 by an informal group of Palestinian academics and intellectuals. It called on scholars across the globe to "refrain from participation in any form of academic and cultural cooperation, collaboration or joint projects with Israeli institutions;" to "advocate a comprehensive boycott of Israeli institutions;" to "promote divestment and disinvestment from Israel by international academic institutions;" to "work toward the condemnation of Israeli policies by pressing for resolutions to be adopted by academic, professional and cultural associations and organizations;" and to "support Palestinian academic and cultural institutions directly without requiring them to partner with Israeli counterparts."

The following year the British Association of University Teachers announced it would boycott two Israeli institutions. Although that boycott was eventually abandoned, the move prompted the AAUP to issue a statement condemning academic boycotts. It rejected "proposals that curtail the freedom of teachers and researchers to engage in work with academic colleagues, and . . . reaffirm[ed] the paramount importance of the freest possible international movement of scholars and ideas." A longer statement, *On Academic Boycotts*, issued the following year, reiterated that position and addressed counter-arguments, concluding,

> Colleges and universities should be what they purport to be: institutions committed to the search for truth and its free expression. Members of the academic community should feel no obligation to support or contribute to institutions that are not free or that sail under false colors, that is, claim to be free but in fact suppress freedom. Such institutions should not be boycotted. Rather, they should be exposed for what they are, and, wherever possible, the continued exchange of ideas should be actively encouraged. The need is always for more academic freedom, not less.

On Academic Boycotts also recognized "the right of individual faculty members or groups of academics not to cooperate with other individual faculty members or academic institutions with whom or with which they disagree."[23]

Since then the AAUP has consistently held that academic boycotts, including the academic boycott of Israel, violate academic freedom, but that individual faculty members have the right to advocate and participate in such boycotts. In 2013, the association unsuccessfully urged members of the American Studies Association to reject a resolution endorsing the academic boycott of Israel. The next year, however, it opposed legislation that would "prohibit public colleges and universities from using state funds to support academic organizations that have passed resolutions or taken official actions to promote boycotts against higher education institutions in other countries." In 2018, Committee A issued a statement decrying laws in at least seventeen states that require government contractors to pledge they do not support BDS. Some universities reportedly required speakers invited to campus and external reviewers of tenure and promotion materials to sign such a pledge. At the University of Houston, a translator filed suit after he was denied payment for work he had already completed after he refused to sign the pledge.[24]

"Academic freedom is meaningless if it does not protect those who support unpopular positions, including the advocacy of academic boycotts. If controversial political issues such as the Israeli-Palestinian conflict cannot be freely discussed and debated in institutions of higher education, where can such debate and discussion occur? We urge opponents of academic boycotts to engage boycott advocates in dialogue, rather than seek to impose inappropriate restrictions on their activities that violate principles of academic freedom," the AAUP declared.[25]

Of particular concern are two McCarthy-like blacklists of pro-BDS advocates, the AMCHA Initiative and Canary Mission. The former is "dedicated to investigating, documenting, educating about, and combating antisemitism at institutions of higher education in America." In 2014, it published a list of 218 faculty members in Middle Eastern Studies at US colleges and universities who signed a petition supporting an academic boycott of Israel, calling on people to "share this list with your family, friends, and associates." The organization asked, "How can professors who are so biased against the Jewish state accurately or fairly teach students about Israel or the Arab-Israel conflict?" But the very nature of the conflict in the Middle East mandates honest scholars to draw conclusions that others may perceive as taking sides. The notion that students should not take classes from teachers with a bias, anti-Israel or other, demonstrated by their extramural expression—and by "bias" what is really meant is a political position that differs from those making this charge—insults those teachers and infantilizes students. Canary Mission maintains a database of "people and groups that are promoting hatred of the USA, Israel and the Jewish people, particularly on college campuses in North America." It lists contact information as well as names, thus facilitating harassment. The site also posts names and information on undergraduate students as well as professors, the clear intention being to hinder admission of these activists to graduate programs. Opposing a boycott by creating a blacklist is nothing short of perverse.[26]

In 2018, a professor at the University of Michigan who supports the BDS movement rescinded an offer to write a letter of recommendation for a student who wished to study in Israel. The university administration disciplined him without an appropriate faculty hearing, prompting the AAUP to write in his support. An online petition demanded his dismissal, and he received death threats. Others supported his action, and nearly everyone agreed that the university's policy was imprecise and difficult to enforce.

But the underlying question remains. Should a professor have the right to deny a recommendation to a student on the basis, not of the student's qualifications, but on that of the professor's personal disapproval of the program to which the student is applying? Faculty members have a general professional obligation to write letters of recommendation for students, but no one should be obliged to write any specific recommendation. Clearly, it is both permissible and often wise for faculty members to decline invitations to write on behalf of students whom they believe unqualified or unsuited or with whom they are not sufficiently familiar to write anything meaningful, or simply owing to time constraints. But is a professor's support for the academic boycott of Israel sufficient justification for denying a recommendation to a student wishing to study there, implicitly attempting to impose the boycott on an unwilling participant?

The professor's supporters responded to such questions by arguing that instructors "have the ethical responsibility to stand by our political convictions, to advance social justice, and to expose falsehoods and partial truths" and that they are entitled to "act in a manner that conforms to their stated positions." These are, indeed, ethical responsibilities, but they cannot readily be disentangled from the faculty's professional responsibilities to treat students fairly and not discriminate against those with whom they disagree. If we permit faculty in all cases to "act in a manner that conforms" to their beliefs and positions, what are we to do about, say, an evangelical Protestant professor who declines to write a recommendation for a student seeking admission to a Catholic institution? Might a conservative professor be justified in denying activist liberal or leftist students services offered willingly to others?

Faculty members have the right to decline to write a recommendation, but they should take into consideration standards of professional ethics and strive not to make decisions that would effectively discriminate against a student for that student's views or personal choices. This is not only a matter of ethics but of student rights. As the 1967 *Joint Statement on the Rights and Freedoms of Students* stated, "Student performance should be evaluated solely on an academic basis, not on opinions or conduct in matters unrelated to academic standards." A 1970 AAUP statement titled *Freedom and Responsibility* declared that "most faculty members face no insoluble conflicts between the claims of politics, social action, and conscience, on the one hand, and the claims and expectations of their students, colleagues, and institutions, on the other. If such conflicts become acute, and attention to obligations as a citizen and moral agent precludes an instructor from fulfilling substantial academic obligations, the instructor cannot escape the responsibility of that choice."[27]

Who Speaks for the Institution?

The 1940 *Statement* encourages professors, in their extramural expression, to "make every effort to indicate that they are not speaking for the institution." As a general rule, all public comments made by faculty members as citizens, whether controversial, indisputable, or merely innocuous, never speak for the institution. That should always be clear. Hence an administration need not, and in most cases should not, publicly criticize a professor's controversial views. Because colleges and universities are devoted to the unfettered search for truth, as institutions there are very few things on which they should take "official" positions. Consider, for example, the theory of evolution. If asked whether a university endorses the theory, in principle an appropriate response of a university president might be that the institution has no official position, but that its scientists all embrace the theory. To be sure, institutions of higher education can and should publicly endorse some basic principles requisite to the pursuit of their mission, not least of all academic freedom. But even here administrators should exercise caution. Each time a college or university administrator publicly passes judgment on behalf of the institution on the extramural expression of an individual faculty member, that administrator effectively takes an "official" position on the issue at hand. There may well be instances in which such statements are unavoidable, but if this becomes a habit, it is not very difficult to see the problems ahead.

When, in 2018, the campus chancellors of the University of California system issued a joint statement condemning the academic boycott of Israel as a "direct and serious threat to academic freedom," some Berkeley faculty members wrote to Chancellor Carol Christ to complain that "for the Chancellors to take a side in such a political debate can only have a chilling effect on campus speech, especially giving faculty pause as they consider taking a public position that is well within the purview of their academic freedom." Christ replied that she was exercising her own individual academic freedom.

But to what extent may university administrators claim individual academic freedom? In 2020, a vocal BDS supporter was appointed interim dean of the Elliott School of International Affairs at George Washington University after having served as vice-dean. Opposition came swiftly. A petition demanded that the school "select a better-suited candidate for the permanent dean." That demand was met when the provost announced that the interim dean would not be a candidate for the permanent position. One of the interim dean's critics asked, "Is being a supporter of academic boycotts of Israel consistent with holding an administrative position such as being a dean?" It's a legitimate question, especially in this case, since deans are often responsible for approving and coordinating international collaborations. Unfortunately, the preemptive removal of the interim dean's name from the permanent search prevented the question from being properly considered at GWU.

For some, signing a pledge not "to collaborate on projects and events involving Israeli academic institutions" goes beyond a personal commitment to BDS. "Such a commitment is much more than an expression of an academic view," wrote one BDS critic who also defends the academic freedom of BDS supporters. "It is a stated intention to violate the academic freedom of others—which is absolutely inconsistent with holding an administrative position at an American university. A dean—even an interim dean—cannot perform her job if she has announced in advance that she will not collaborate with other academic institutions on the basis of nationality." But another commentator wrote, "Assuming that anyone who makes a personal pledge or commitment will therefore impose that pledge on the institution they work for is a disturbing argument. If a religious person made a pledge to promote their religious values, should they be banned from all administrative positions on the assumption that a dean would use their role to impose their religion on everyone?"[28]

Candidates for a faculty appointment or an administrative position must be judged only by their fitness for the position, their qualifications. Should advocacy of a position that runs counter to principles of academic freedom be treated as disqualifying? Perhaps, but only if there is evidence to suggest the candidate has taken or clearly will take inappropriate actions. People should be held accountable for what they *do*, not what others may, with or without good reason, *fear* they might do on the basis of their extramural comments.

One implication of this controversy was the suggestion that only faculty should have academic freedom; those in administrative positions with academic responsibilities should not. Whether academic administrators have an academic freedom right to extramural expression was addressed in an instructive 2018 investigation of McGill University by the Canadian Association of University Teachers (CAUT). When the director of the McGill Institute for the Study of Canada published an article in a popular magazine labeling the province of Quebec "an almost pathologically alienated and low-trust society, deficient in many of the most basic forms of social capital that other Canadians take for granted," McGill was inundated with calls for his removal, and he soon resigned his directorship under pressure. When faculty members voiced concerns about academic freedom, McGill "took the position that the protections of academic freedom did not extend to academic administrators. Over the course of several weeks, the University developed and promoted a theory of the conditional academic freedom of academic administrators which both purported to justify [the] resignation and put other administrators on notice that their academic freedom was subject to limits."

The CAUT investigation report subjected this doctrine to withering critique. It declared:

There is no valid distinction to be made between the academic freedom rights of academic administrators and those of all other members of the faculty. Consequently, academics who serve as administrators must be able to rely on the same protections in their academic activities as administrators that they would enjoy were they in non-administrative academic positions. And that protection must be seen to cover all of their activities, both intramural and extramural, so that they are not treated any differently as administrators with respect to academic freedom than they would be if they were academic staff without administrative duties.

The fundamental point here is that the university is not a workplace like any other, where managerial conformity or corporate reputation must be maintained by gag rules that assure administrative unity of practice or discourse. Instead, the university is understood as a space where gag rules themselves must be prohibited in the interest of protecting the institution's fundamental commitment to the search for "knowledge and understanding" which requires an environment where there is no place for "institutional censorship." . . .

Administrators will certainly be constrained in their personal academic work if they know that, should their writings or other forms of expression cause a hostile public outcry, they could be judged to have created a "negative impact" and to have failed to uphold the mission of the unit they administer. . . . [The McGill leadership's theory] makes it highly likely that those who become administrators will be conformist bureaucrats with little taste or capacity for the critical commentary and engagement necessary for academic life.[29]

In short, administrators with academic responsibilities—for instance, deans or program directors but not necessarily those without such responsibilities, such as the campus police chief or the comptroller—should be entitled to the same academic freedom rights as faculty members with regard to their extramural expression. Such expression should only be relevant when it bears upon the individual's fitness for the position. Criteria of fitness for an administrative position, however, may differ from those for a strictly faculty position.

Political Activity

Is it appropriate for professors to run for political office or otherwise be involved in government or political organizations? That was a question the authors of the 1915 *Declaration* thought "deserving of consideration" but which they declined to answer. They believed it was "manifestly desirable that such teachers have minds untrammeled by party loyalties, unexcited by party enthusiasms, and unbiased by personal political ambitions; and that universities should remain uninvolved in party antagonisms. On the other hand, it is equally manifest that the material available for the service of the state would be restricted in a highly undesirable way, if it were understood that no member of the academic profession should ever be called upon to assume the responsibilities of public office."

Over the next several decades, professors ran for public office or were otherwise engaged in political activity without visible conflict with the principles of academic freedom, perhaps because, as C. Wright Mills would claim in 1951, "as a group, American professors have seldom if ever been politically engaged."[30] To be sure, there were multiple cases in which the political views of faculty members played a prominent role, but it was not until the anti-Communist hysteria of the 1950s that political affiliation itself became a central issue. At the time some—most famously the philosopher Sidney Hook—argued that Communists could not think independently and had to obey Communist Party orders, thereby sacrificing their academic freedom, which justified their removal if they declined to renounce Communist affiliations.[31] In 1956, in a special report, *Academic Freedom and Tenure in the Quest for National Security*, the AAUP belatedly reviewed many of the cases from the earlier part of the decade in which faculty members had been dismissed for refusing to deny or reveal past or present membership in the Communist Party. The report concluded that only "conscious participation in conspiracy against the government" could justify removal.[32]

In 1969, the AAUP approved the *Statement on Professors and Political Activity*, which was endorsed the following year by the AAC. It spelled out five principles governing faculty political activity. First, as citizens, faculty members "should be free to engage in political activities so far as they are able to do so consistently with their obligations as teachers and scholars." Second, while "many kinds of political activity . . . are consistent with effective service as members of the faculty," others "will often require that professors seek a leave of absence." Third, institutions should provide arrangements to facilitate such activity "similar to those applicable to other public or private extramural service," including reductions in workload and "equitable adjustment of compensation." Fourth, those "seeking leaves should recognize that they have a primary obligation to their institution and to their growth as educators and scholars." Fifth, "a leave of absence incident to political activity should come under the institution's normal rules and regulations for leaves of absence" and "not affect unfavorably the tenure status of a faculty member."[33]

What if a faculty member's government service becomes controversial, raising questions about fitness to return to the classroom? When John Yoo, a tenured University of California law professor, took a leave of absence to work in the George W. Bush administration, his work involved justifying enhanced interrogation techniques widely condemned as torture. When he returned to the university there were calls for his removal. Lacking evidence of "clear professional misconduct," the faculty and administration declined to act. Scott Atlas, a former member of the Stanford University medical faculty and a fellow of the Hoover Institution, served as the Trump administration's chief advocate for herd immunity in response to the COVID-19 pandemic. The Stanford Faculty Senate passed a resolution declaring that his "disdain for established medical knowledge violates medical ethics defined by the American Medical Association" and that his "behavior is anathema to our community, our values, and our belief that we should use knowledge for good." Academic freedom should surely protect Atlas's views as a citizen, but faculty members were suggesting that he had abused his White House position by implying that he was a qualified medical professional in the field (he is a radiologist, not an expert in either infectious disease or epidemiology). Still, the resolution did not call for disciplinary action. At Harvard, an open letter circulated among students, faculty, and staff calling on the university to develop "accountability guidelines" for inviting former members of the Trump administration to campus as professors, fellows, or speakers.[34]

Should controversial government service by academics always be protected by academic freedom? The answer is not entirely clear, because policy making may straddle the border between extramural expression and professional scholarly activity. Nonetheless, the bar must be set high in determining whether or not judgments about such service are relevant to a faculty member's fitness to teach or conduct research.

Intramural Expression

Neither the 1915 *Declaration* nor the 1940 *Statement* carved out a unique place for what is often called freedom of intramural expression, "faculty speech that does not involve disciplinary expertise but is instead about the action, policy, or personnel of a faculty member's institution."[35] But the *Statement*'s claim that "teachers are citizens, members of a learned profession, and *officers of an educational institution*" (emphasis added) can be said to serve that function. The thrust of this phrase is to link closely faculty members' rights as citizens and professionals with obligations to participate in the life of their institutions. Previously, the 1915 *Declaration* had proposed that with respect to an institution's trustees, "faculties hold an *independent* place, with quite *equal* responsibilities," and hence must be seen as "the appointees, but not in any proper sense the employees" of those trustees.

These principles would be spelled out more fully in the 1966 joint *Statement on Government of Colleges and Universities,* which defined the system of shared governance and acknowledged the faculty's "primary responsibility" in curricular matters and faculty status, as well as aspects of student life related to the curriculum, and posited that its authority should normally be respected by the administration (see chapter 1), a standard now embraced by most colleges and universities—albeit too often more in theory than in practice. In 1994, the AAUP adopted *On the Relationship of Faculty Governance to Academic Freedom,* which addressed the links between shared governance arrangements and academic freedom. It argued that "a sound system of institutional governance is a necessary condition for the protection of faculty rights and thereby for the most productive exercise of essential faculty freedoms. Correspondingly, the protection of the academic freedom of faculty members in addressing issues of institutional governance is a prerequisite for the practice of governance unhampered by fear of retribution." The statement argued that the faculty's academic freedom must encompass the right to express views "on matters having to do with their institution and its policies" because "grounds for thinking an institutional policy desirable or undesirable must be heard and assessed if the community is to have confidence that its policies are appropriate." The statement continued, "Protecting academic freedom on campus requires ensuring that a particular instance of faculty speech will be subject to discipline only where that speech violates some central principle of academic morality" and "clearly supports a judgment of competence or incompetence."[36]

While faculty members may be subject to disciplinary action by administrators in accordance with these principles, it must be unambiguous that faculty members are neither *subordinate* to, nor do they *report* to, members of the administration. It is therefore not the role of faculty members to obey administrative directives or demonstrate loyalty to administrative initiatives or to individual administrators or trustees. It is a faculty member's right not only to disagree with administrative decisions but also to criticize them, either explicitly or implicitly, without fear of retaliation or reprimand. (Unfortunately, legal protection for such disagreement or criticism has been somewhat eroded at public institutions by the US Supreme Court's 2006 ruling in *Garcetti v. Ceballos*, discussed in chapter 6).

In 1927, the University of Louisville's president dismissed the historian Louis Gottschalk for lack of "loyalty." The AAUP investigating committee responded, "The sort of 'loyalty' which President Colvin seems to have demanded is not loyalty, but subservience. . . . The Committee cannot too strongly condemn the attempt to introduce such a conception of 'loyalty' into the administration of a reputable college or university."

In 1933, the AAUP investigated the dismissal of senior faculty members at Rollins College in Florida. At the time the school was considered one of the leading progressive institutions in the country, but its president governed much like an autocrat, backed by his trustees. "If there is as much as fifty percent disagreement between me and any member of the faculty on fundamental matters," he declared, "either [the faculty member] or I should go." When a group of faculty members raised questions about a series of presidential decisions on curriculum and faculty rights, the response was thus to summarily dismiss the group's outspoken leader, classicist John Rice, and then others.

The AAUP investigation was led by none other than Arthur Lovejoy, indicating the case's potential importance. Dismissing Rice's "frequently vehement, sometimes intemperate, and in several instances discourteous language" and his "sometimes inopportune humor" as simple "errors of judgment and . . . of taste," Lovejoy's report explained that while academic freedom must protect against "infringements on theological, political, economic, and social thought," it must also protect "educational" thought. The report concluded that in rejecting the "prerogative of faculty members to exercise professional responsibilities in educational matters" and denying their freedom from disciplinary consequences when expressing views on institutional affairs, the Rollins president and board violated academic freedom.[37]

Freedom of intramural expression must also include the freedom to organize faculty members to exert their collective power, including through a union. While the National Labor Relations Act in the private sector, and most state legislation establishing a public employee right to unionize formally protect workers from retaliation for union activity, those protections may be breached as frequently in higher education as they so often are in other sectors. Such breaches may not only sometimes be illegal, but they are *always* infringements on academic freedom. Ever since the Supreme Court ruled in 1980 that most tenure-track professors in private colleges and universities are "managers" and hence ineligible for protection under the NLRA (see chapter 6), most faculty union organizing has focused on faculty on term contracts—so-called adjuncts—and in public institutions in states where collective bargaining for such faculties is legally established. But even where collective bargaining is not protected by statute, faculty members should have unfettered rights to discuss institutional matters in meetings outside those established by the institution; distribute union and other professional literature; wear buttons, tee shirts, and similar paraphernalia promoting a union or cause; circulate and sign petitions; and join together to protest and change institutional policies and practices.

Since "there should be no invidious distinctions between those who teach and/or conduct research in higher education, regardless of whether they hold full-time or part-time appointments or whether their appointments are tenured, tenure-track, or contingent," freedom of intramural expression must adhere as well to those off the tenure-track.[38] In 2016, a part-time community college philosophy instructor drafted a letter to his school's accrediting agency, complaining about a new curriculum that had been imposed on him. Within a week he had been summarily dismissed mid-semester, ostensibly for "instructional deficiencies so severe that they necessitated [his] immediate removal." An AAUP investigation found that rationale "strains credulity." More likely, the dismissal was "a gross violation of his right to intramural speech under principles of academic freedom," a charge left unrefuted since the instructor had no access to even a weak grievance mechanism.

A shrewder administration might have let the instructor "finish the semester and then have declined to renew his contract," the investigation pointed out. That "would have constituted just as severe a violation of academic freedom. But the administration would have enjoyed the plausible deniability afforded by policies and procedures that enshrine arbitrary nonrenewal of appointments for adjunct faculty members." The investigation concluded, "The private business model of academic employment, in which managers exercise complete control over the working conditions and appointment status of those they oversee, is already a reality for the majority of those who teach at US colleges and universities."[39]

There is good reason to suspect that nonrenewals for unstated motives in violation of academic freedom are regular occurrences at all levels of higher education today. How often are teachers simply informed without explanation that there is no longer work for them or that their assignments have been drastically reduced—sometimes leaving them ineligible for health insurance—owing, in reality, to unsubstantiated student complaints, reports of an ill-conceived or ill-timed Facebook post, a complaint about institutional policies, or suspected union sympathies? While such actions may be mitigated by union contracts, which now cover about a fifth of those teaching in higher education, vulnerability to pretextual nonrenewals remains high even among the unionized. That is why the massive erosion of the tenure system since the mid-1970s has become by far the single gravest threat to academic freedom.

Chapter 5

Tenure

Tenure is frequently derided as an elitist and selfish privilege, a "professional masquerade," to use constitutional law scholar and former AAUP president William Van Alstyne's phrase. It has been charged with being an obstacle to efficiency, accountability, and reform; a protection for mediocrity and academic "dead wood"; and a barrier to the emergence of the new, the fresh, and the young. Mythic tales of burned-out tenured professors droning and mumbling through lectures based on decades-old notes abound. Even when a tenured faculty member stands accused of serious and unprofessional, even criminal, misconduct—sexual harassment, for example—tenure is often claimed to render him untouchable. But since tenure is as much misunderstood as maligned, as Van Alstyne noted, its "best defense may well inhere simply in a clear statement of what it is—and what it is not."[1]

Tenure Defined

To turn briefly to what tenure is not, despite common misunderstanding, it is *not* a guarantee of lifetime employment, nor is it designed to shield misconduct or incompetence. Firing a tenured professor is not only possible; it happens more than occasionally. Moreover, even though such dismissals rightly place a high burden of proof on an institution, in more than a handful of cases tenured instructors faced with the threat of dismissal choose instead to retire or quietly resign.

The 1940 *Statement* declares, "Tenure is a means to certain ends; specifically: (1) freedom of teaching and research and of extramural activities, and (2) a sufficient degree of economic security to make the profession attractive to men and women of ability. Freedom and economic security, hence, tenure, are indispensable to the success of an institution in fulfilling its obligations to its students and to society."

The *Statement* offers this definition of tenure: "After the expiration of a probationary period, teachers or investigators should have permanent or continuous tenure, and their service should be terminated only for adequate cause, except in the case of retirement for age, or under extraordinary circumstances because of financial exigencies." The probationary period is then defined as not to "exceed seven years, including within this period full-time service in all institutions of higher education." (Since most institutions, in accordance with AAUP guidelines, provide a year's notice if tenure is to be denied, for practical purposes this period will often amount to six years.) The *Statement* adds that "during the probationary period a teacher should have the academic freedom that all other members of the faculty have." With respect to termination of an appointment, it calls for due process protections and a hearing before a faculty committee. It also notes that a termination "because of financial exigency should be demonstrably bona fide."

Three important observations must be made about this definition.

First, tenure need not be granted on the basis of a formal and rigorous review process, although most institutions with tenure systems sensibly require such a process. It can be acquired automatically, when a faculty member reaches the end of the requisite period of full-time service. If the 1940 *Statement* is to apply, as soon as that term is complete a faculty member will be entitled to the privileges of tenure, irrespective of institutional action. This is why the AAUP does not recognize any type of full-time appointment other than probationary for tenure or tenured, regardless of the contractual or legal position an individual faculty member may occupy within a given institution's policies.

Second, tenure is not limited to those who may hold a specific academic rank or title. It may be granted to assistant, associate, or full professors or to instructors and lecturers or to so-called professors of practice. Nor is tenure a reward for merit or a symbol of prestige. It simply denotes a continuing appointment, not professional standing. While many institutions prioritize research as a criterion for awarding tenure, its purpose is to ensure academic freedom and security in *all* professional duties. It protects both research and teaching. Indeed, the high water mark of tenure's reach came in the 1960s and early '70s, with the immense growth of community colleges and state technical and teacher-training institutions, where the great majority of faculty positions were devoted exclusively or almost exclusively to teaching, yet still carried with them the prospect of tenure.

Third—and this is the most critical point—tenure provides that once a probationary period is complete, a full-time faculty member may be dismissed only for *adequate cause* or only on account of bona fide financial exigency or program discontinuance. What is meant by "adequate cause?" The AAUP has largely left this to individual institutions to determine, but in 1973 a joint Commission on Academic Tenure in Higher Education, sponsored by the AAUP and the AACU, recommended that grounds for dismissal be limited to "(a) demonstrated incompetence or dishonesty in teaching or research, (b) substantial and manifest neglect of duty, and (c) personal conduct which substantially impairs the individual's fulfillment of his [or her] institutional responsibilities."[2] The latter might well include demonstrated sexual harassment or other blatantly discriminatory behavior. In the course of its investigations and policy development, the AAUP has deemed a number of grounds for dismissal inadmissible, however, including insubordination, political affiliation, damaging the reputation of the institution, or the mere fact of negative performance reviews.

As Matthew Finkin points out, unique to tenure is "the requirement of a hearing by one's academic peers before the dismissal may occur."[3] Tenure is thus essentially a guarantee of due process and presumption of innocence. The procedural protections associated with tenure, outlined in the 1940 *Statement* and described more fully in the AAUP's *Recommended Institutional Regulations on Academic Freedom and Tenure* and in the 1958 joint AAUP and AAC *Statement on Procedural Standards in Faculty Dismissal Proceedings*, can be viewed as analogous to fair hearing requirements and statutory protections in public sector employment and to grievance procedures in many collective bargaining agreements.

Van Alstyne offered this summary of what tenure means:

> The conferral of tenure means that the institution, after utilizing a probationary period of as long as six years in which it has had ample opportunity to determine the professional competence and responsibility of its appointees, has rendered a favorable judgment establishing a rebuttable presumption of the individual's professional excellence. As the lengthy term of probationary service will have provided the institution with sufficient experience to determine whether the faculty member is worthy of a presumption of professional fitness, it has not seemed unreasonable to shift to the individual the benefit of doubt when the institution thereafter extends his service beyond the period of probation and, correspondingly, to shift to the institution the obligation fairly to show why, if at all, that faculty member should nonetheless be

fired. The presumption of the tenured faculty member's professional excellence thus remains rebuttable, exactly to the extent that when it can be shown that the individual possessing tenure has nonetheless fallen short or has otherwise misconducted himself as determined according to full academic due process, the presumption is lost and the individual is subject to dismissal.[4]

As with academic freedom in general, tenure is not designed first and foremost to provide protection to individual scholars. The 1940 *Statement* recognized that colleges and universities "are conducted for the common good and not to further the interest of either the individual teacher or the institution as a whole." Academic freedom and tenure, therefore, "do not exist because of a peculiar solicitude for the human beings who staff our academic institutions."[5] Tenure protects academic freedom by ensuring that scholars may be uninhibited in criticizing and advocating controversial changes in accepted theories, widely held beliefs, existing institutions, as well as the policies, programs, and leadership of their own institutions. But perhaps most important, the existence of a sufficiently large group of tenured faculty can ensure that dissenters and gadflies can have a community of supporters able to advocate on their behalf. As the libertarian economist and former AAUP president Fritz Machlup put it, "We need and want teachers and scholars who would unhesitatingly come to the defense of the 'odd ball,' the heretic, the dissenter, the troublemaker, whose freedom to speak and to write is under some threat from colleagues, administrators, governing board, government, or pressure groups. The impulse to take up the cudgels for the 'odd ball' is all too easily suppressed if unpleasant consequences must be feared by those who defend him."

Sadly, it must be acknowledged that such defenders, even among the tenured, are often hard to come by—far too many are timid, fearful, and cowed. The 2011 AAUP statement, *Ensuring Academic Freedom in Politically Controversial Academic Personnel*

Decisions, acknowledged that "mere adherence to due process or weak or substantively biased faculty committees may provide politicized decision making with a veneer of legitimacy. . . . [A]lthough procedural protections . . . are crucial to the defense of academic freedom, they may not be sufficient in themselves, especially in cases where the dissenting faculty member confronts a strong mainstream consensus in support of repression."[6] As the ranks of the tenured thin, that problem only worsens. Still, as Ralph Brown and Jordan Kurland put it, "there is some truth, as well as considerable paternalism, in the statement that the best protection for the academic freedom of the nontenured is a strong tenured faculty."

If, in addition to its protection of academic freedom, tenure is designed to secure "a sufficient degree of economic security to make the profession attractive," its assurance of long-term employment stability provides an important benefit to both the tenured faculty and their institutions. Economists have long known that stable employment promotes efficiency by diminishing uncertainty, a perception that seems unfortunately lost on many employers in today's "gig economy." It also benefits the institution by ensuring that faculty who in practice make hiring and tenure decisions are not threatened by the advance of younger colleagues.

It used to be argued that tenure offered a tradeoff between long-term security and higher salaries. The existence of tenure was said to keep professorial salaries lower than they would be without the system. Individual professors could earn more on the job market were they to sacrifice the security of tenure, it was said. Machlup, who studied the "economics of knowledge," quoted one tenure critic as follows: "If I had a man on for 15, 20, or 25 years—not knowing whether in the long run he would be worth it but having to pay him month in and month out as long as he was doing a passable job, and couldn't dismiss him, my tendency would be to pay him as little as possible."[7] For many years the belief—that while tenure's prospect of job security might attract some to academia, it also tended to reduce salaries—was not questioned by economists, although it was a principle derived from theoretical assumptions and not based on data.

Today that thesis is laughable. Now that only a fourth of those teaching in higher education have access to a tenure system, we can readily compare the salaries of those in the system with those who are not. It's no contest, no matter how much salaries of tenured faculty have stagnated in recent years. Studies find that part-time faculty earn about 60 percent less than comparable full-time tenure-track faculty for the same or more work. Median salaries of full-time non-tenure-track faculty twenty years ago were roughly 25-30 percent lower than those of full-time tenure-track faulty, although that gap has since narrowed a bit. The same can be said of faculty whose assignment is fully in research, especially the burgeoning ranks of those on postdocs.[8]

Financial Exigency and Program Discontinuance

In addition to dismissal for cause, tenured faculty members may, according to the terms of the 1940 *Statement,* be let go in cases of bona fide financial exigency or program discontinuance. As public funding of higher education has steadily and at times dramatically declined, and many private institutions have also found themselves in dire financial straits, claims of financial exigency and efforts to reduce costs by eliminating programs have increased. In such cases the dismissal of tenured faculty may be the only solution available. If there are adverse implications for academic freedom, these will depend on the fairness with which the layoffs are administered. In many—perhaps most—instances, however, such actions are not warranted; other mechanisms to deal with fiscal challenges are available, and financial concerns may be little more than a pretext for getting rid of allegedly unproductive, unpopular, or troublesome professors or for realigning programmatic offerings to suit the perceived preferences of politicians, donors, trustees, or academic administrators themselves. As US appellate court Judge Skelly Wright recognized in 1975, "financial exigency can become too easy an excuse for dismissing a teacher who is merely unpopular or controversial or misunderstood . . . without according him his important procedural rights."[9]

The AAUP defines a bona fide financial exigency as "a severe financial crisis that fundamentally compromises the academic integrity of the institution as a whole and that cannot be alleviated by less drastic means" than the termination of tenured faculty appointments.[10] That definition was formulated in a lengthy 2013 report, *The Role of the Faculty in Conditions of Financial Exigency*, which elaborated that the

> definition names a condition that is less dramatic than that in which the very existence of the institution is immediately in jeopardy but is vastly more serious and threatening to the academic integrity of the institution than ordinary (short- and long-term) attrition in operating budgets. Financial exigency can legitimately be declared only when the institution's academic integrity will be fundamentally compromised by prolonged and drastic reductions in funds available to the institution and only when the determination of the institution's financial health is guided by generally accepted accounting principles. In proposing this new definition, however, we insist that financial exigency is not a plausible complaint from a campus that has shifted resources from its primary missions of teaching and research toward the employment of increasing numbers of administrators or toward unnecessary capital expenditures.

With respect to program discontinuances, the report acknowledged that "a college or university can discontinue a program of instruction, but our standard has been that if the discontinuation is not undertaken for financial reasons, it must be shown to enhance the educational mission of the institution as a whole; we have long acknowledged that programs can be cut in times of financial exigency, but only if an appropriate faculty body is involved in the decision-making process, beginning with the determination of whether an institution is experiencing bona fide financial exigency." The report added, "An institution's desire to shift priorities is not the same as a fiscal crisis, and one should not mistake the former for the latter."[11]

The 2013 report came in response to a series of threatened or actual program discontinuances and layoffs in New York, Louisiana, Nevada, Iowa, and Illinois in the aftermath of the 2008 financial crisis, several of which involved layoffs of tenured faculty members. However, the issue was not new. Soon after release of the 1940 *Statement*, the AAUP investigated dismissals of tenured faculty owing to claims of exigency at Adelphi College (now Adelphi University) in 1939 and Memphis State College (now the University of Memphis) in 1942. In the 1970s, the association witnessed a wave of cases involving declarations of financial exigency. At that time, as in more recent times, "the financial crisis was real—and deep." Frequently, however, the AAUP's "investigations found that institutional authorities declared financial exigency under circumstances that bordered on the ludicrous. . . . Then as now, 'crises' were announced as pretexts for decisions that effectively eroded the institution of tenure; then as now, those decisions were made almost entirely without faculty input or consultation."

Three examples of financial exigency from three decades are illustrative.

In 1975, the City University of New York experienced, as a consequence of the city's drastic fiscal crisis, an extraordinary budget reduction of nearly 20 percent, exacerbated by the high inflation rates of that era. The result, the CUNY chancellor told the *New York Times,* was that "we took a thousand people we had given contracts to for September and told them we could not honor them. We gave them thirty-day notices." The AAUP appointed a special investigating committee. Its lengthy report was unable to determine "whether among the thousand full-time and the roughly five thousand part-time faculty who were separated from the University there were any cases where the claim of exigency masked violations of academic freedom." Nor were any tenured faculty dismissed, although "about ten professors who were informed that they would be granted tenure were terminated before" their tenured status could commence. The investigation did find that CUNY leaders had "disregarded the interest in having a reasonable period of notice for those faculty members who faced retrenchment" and that "the machinery for faculty participation in the central decisions of the University is intrinsically and chronically inadequate."[12]

In 1992, 111 tenured professors and 35 probationary faculty members at San Diego State University were informed that "because of lack of funds or lack of work" they would be laid off. Under intense pressure from faculty, students, and eventually the leadership of the California State University system itself, the layoff notices were rescinded. The AAUP investigated anyway, "because the effort to terminate the appointments of tenured faculty on such a scale is historically unprecedented, because these events illuminate the significance of tenure—and of sound academic government—in a time of financial stress, and because many of the institutional concerns which gave rise to the decisions at San Diego State remained." With respect to tenure, the SDSU president had acknowledged that the university's financial problems could be addressed without resorting to dismissal of tenured faculty, but that "would have posed an obstacle to other institutional ends which to him were more deserving." Among those ends was a claim to necessary "personnel flexibility." Since this claim is frequently heard from administrations seeking either to remove tenured professors or to reduce the proportion of the faculty eligible for tenure, it is worth quoting the investigating committee's response. The president "had it exactly right," they wrote. "Tenure is a limit on the institution's ability to adjust to a reduced budget in any way it seeks. The presidents and faculty members who drafted the 1940 *Statement* thought the limit to be necessary" to achieve that statement's proclaimed ends of protecting academic freedom and providing reasonable job security. With regard to academic freedom, the committee concluded,

> It is unsurprising that in the wake of the disregard for the protections of tenure at SDSU charges of violation of academic freedom have been made: that intramural vendettas were settled, that departments were singled out for deeper cuts to reach outspoken critics of the administration. We have not attempted to assess these charges. We suspect, given the manner in which the decisions were made, that the allegations cannot be proved. Nor, for that same reason, can they be disproved. The disregard of tenure has placed the administration under a cloud of suspicion which, by the very methods it employed, cannot be dispelled; and that fact has contributed significantly to the atmosphere of distrust on the campus.[13]

In 2013, National Louis University, a private institution in Chicago, discontinued nine degree programs and five non-degree certificate programs, closed departments of English and philosophy, fine arts, mathematics, and natural sciences, and terminated the appointments of at least sixty-three full-time faculty members, sixteen with continuous tenure. The university's president claimed that "serious fiscal pressures on the university" and a significant decline in enrollment required taking action "immediately." The administration did not declare financial exigency, however, nor were its decisions preceded by any demonstration that the magnitude of the problems mandated the measures taken. A consultant brought in by concerned faculty found that the university was not in "dire financial condition: there are sufficient reserves and a low level of debt, in addition to solid cash flows in recent years." Moreover, he concluded, terminations of faculty appointments would not save much money and administrative costs had not been addressed. Despite widespread faculty resistance, the program eliminations and layoffs proceeded, resulting, an AAUP investigation concluded, in "the decimation of the full-time faculty." The investigating committee was "struck by how quickly and extensively competent and experienced members of the faculty, many of them with decades of service to the institution, were replaced by a cadre of part-time adjunct faculty members." The report concluded,

> From the standpoint of AAUP principles regarding academic freedom and governance, it can be argued that a department with a faculty consisting largely of adjunct faculty members is not worse off than one consisting of full-time faculty members with a tenure system that has in fact failed to protect tenure and a system of governance in which the administration has been able to reject the decisions of formal faculty bodies. Still, the NLU administration has had to go through certain formalities in order to get around written requirements before it could act as it wishes, but where it has adjunct faculty members serving at its beck and call, it is unfettered in acting summarily. The climate for academic freedom under the current NLU administration may have been precarious for its full-time faculty, but for a faculty serving on part-time appointments, the climate in all likelihood will be lethal.[14]

Michael Bérubé of Pennsylvania State University, the principal author of the 2013 AAUP report, has written that "the most important thing to emphasize about the declaration of exigency is that the faculty must be even more involved in the determination of whether an exigency is real."[15] To that end the *Recommended Institutional Regulations* requires that "as a first step, there should be a faculty body which participates in the decision that a condition of financial exigency exists or is imminent and that all feasible alternatives to termination of appointments have been pursued." The *Regulations* also include a "list of specific alternatives to layoffs that the faculty must make sure have been considered" and mandate that the body is to "not to be appointed by the administration," but "elected."

This book was written while the country reeled from the effects of the 2020 COVID-19 pandemic, with dramatic consequences for higher education finances and pedagogy. By fall 2020, colleges and universities nationwide were suspending or eliminating programs, reducing staff, and laying off or furloughing faculty members, including some with tenure. The U.S. Labor Department estimated in early 2021 that US academic institutions lost a net total of at least 650,000 employees. Put another way, for every eight workers employed in higher education in February 2020, at least one had lost or left that job ten months later. The ranks of dining and residence service workers were decimated. Among faculty, those on contingent contracts were hit especially hard. The consequences of such actions and of subsequent similar actions are likely to be felt for years to come. Enrollment declines were already predicted before the pandemic. Now it is likely that larger institutions may face serious ongoing shortfalls in revenue, while smaller institutions may need to close up shop entirely. In that light attention to these policies on financial exigency, tenure, and academic freedom have become all the more imperative.[16]

Does Tenure Protect "Dead Wood"?

One college president responded to the pandemic by decreeing the elimination of tenure at his institution. "There is an old saying that good faculty don't need it and bad faculty don't deserve it," he explained.[17] Critics of the tenure system often charge that it inappropriately and excessively protects senior faculty who should probably not have been tenured in the first place or, more frequently, have lost enthusiasm for teaching or whose research productivity has stagnated. In short, it is claimed, tenure can promote mediocrity and safeguard "dead wood." No data has ever been offered to suggest that such problems are anything close to widespread, however. In the former case, the rigors of the tenure system and the observance of strict tenure rules actually makes mistakes in hiring and promotion less likely. As for the latter, Fritz Machlup asked, "Is it really believable that many faculty members, once alert, ambitious, inspiring, and productive, but now lazy and dull, would still be live wires, full of spark, and constantly recharged with new learning, if only they had no assured tenure, if only they had to live in constant fear for their jobs? And what about the contrary argument that some people, especially scholars, work much better when they have no worries, no fears?"[18]

This is not to deny, of course, that faculty members, like all people, may change. If some become demoralized or disillusioned, however, might that be a consequence less of tenure than because the leadership of their institutions makes their work more tedious, hidebound by arbitrary rules and paperwork, deprives them of resources, or fails to renew the ranks of their tenure-track colleagues? Making it easier to dismiss such faculty members may do more to exacerbate than solve whatever genuine problems may exist.

One mechanism that many colleges and universities have adopted to address concerns about declining interest and outdated approaches among senior tenured faculty is the post-tenure review. Periodic reviews may prove useful in faculty development, although they may also "generate a good deal of paperwork and take up a great deal of time and energy." In 1983, Harold Shapiro, then president of the University of Michigan and later of Princeton, cautiously endorsed such reviews as "simply good personnel policy," but warned that "we should disconnect such ongoing periodic evaluations from the question of tenure itself. Any attempt to link the issue of tenure and periodic evaluations of tenured faculty, no matter how well-meaning, is, in my judgment, unlikely to strengthen our institutions." In that year the AAUP declared that "periodic formal institutional evaluation of each post-probationary faculty member would bring scant benefit, would incur unacceptable costs, not only in money and time but also in dampening of creativity and of collegial relationships, and would threaten academic freedom." In 1999, the association offered a set of recommended guidelines and standards for post-tenure review systems, adding that "post-tenure review ought to be aimed not at accountability, but at faculty development. Post-tenure review must be developed and carried out by faculty. Post-tenure review must not be a reevaluation of tenure, nor may it be used to shift the burden of proof from an institution's administration (to show cause for dismissal) to the individual faculty member (to show cause why he or she should be retained). Post-tenure review must be conducted according to standards that protect academic freedom and the quality of education."[19]

The Gig Academy

The defense of tenure summarized on the preceding pages largely reiterates arguments crafted between the 1950s and 1980s. During those years, clamorous attacks on tenure seemed to capture a portion of the public's attention every few years, even if these could be of a hit-and-run sort, producing a sustained response that rendered those attacks largely ineffective. One historian found that "in 1935, fewer than half of a sample of seventy-eight universities employed formal tenure policies, and many of these were weak and indeterminate by modern standards. By 1973, almost 100 percent had instituted provisions for tenure."[20] In recent years, however, while some state legislators now and then issue new calls for tenure's elimination—in 2016 proposed legislation to do away with tenure in state universities in Iowa and Missouri failed to win support (as this book was in press such legislation was again under consideration in Iowa)—frontal assaults on the system have by and large yielded to a prolonged and insidious state of siege that has proven far more successful at weakening the tenure system. If we include graduate student instructors, approximately three-fourths of all those who teach in higher education are now employed off the tenure track, compared to only about a fourth forty years ago. At four-year public institutions, 56 percent of full-time and part-time faculty members are off the tenure track; the figure at four-year private institutions is 66 percent.[21]

To be sure, a limited number of part-time appointments without access to tenure can offer a valid mechanism for addressing some curricular needs. According to one survey, about 11 percent of part-timers are actually retired tenured professors. Another 23 percent have career employment outside higher education, perhaps as a practicing nurse, journalist, or attorney. They may teach one or two classes, but their income derives mainly from nonacademic occupations. The remaining 66 percent can be deemed precarious. According to a report by the TIAA Institute, about 70 percent of such "adjuncts" are over forty years old, with a third aged between fifty-five and sixty-nine. Approximately one-half teach one or two courses at a single institution, while 22 percent teach three or more classes at two or more institutions. About one-half say they would prefer a tenure-track position, with an additional 10 percent preferring a full-time non-tenure-track position.

If tenure is a means toward ensuring economic security, the erosion of tenure all but guarantees insecurity. On average, part-time faculty make a full-time equivalent of $22,400 annually—less than most fast-food workers—for teaching eight classes (a bit short of $3,000 per class). Almost 60 percent receive less. The Labor Center at UC Berkeley has reported that a quarter of part-time instructors nationally receive some kind of public assistance. According to the most thorough study, "in no other sector has contingency among high-skill professionals come with such dramatic wage decreases." That study also affirmed that "whatever purpose labor restructuring in higher education has served, it is clearly not being used to make college costs more competitive." Instead, funds previously devoted to instruction have increasingly gone to support the ever-expanding business functions of the university or to non-instructional student services. Executive positions are growing at an especially rapid pace, with salary increases far outpacing those of even the most highly paid tenured faculty.[22]

Reliance on part-time, precarious faculty labor is not confined to teaching. Chapter 2 took note of the growth in full-time research faculty employed on a contingent basis, especially in medical schools and STEM disciplines, and the growing employment of postdocs. One study calculates that since 1980, the postdoc population rose from under 20,000 to around 79,000, with another study estimating the current number at over 90,000. Compounding the problem is that a majority of postdocs are international scholars working on temporary visas, which stipulate ongoing employment, thus making them vulnerable to abuse and discrimination, as well as retaliation for exercising their academic freedom. Many postdocs complain they are denied full or fair authorship on publications to which they have contributed.

If we understand, as this book argues, that academic freedom does not aspire solely, or even mainly, to protect the rights of individual teachers and researchers, but is instead designed to protect the collective freedom of the faculty, then we must ask, as two adjuncts have, "What becomes of that freedom if the vast majority of faculty members cannot exercise their collective functions without fearing employer retribution?" In Colorado's community colleges, the state's AAUP leaders report, "it is not unusual at all for college administrators to simply refuse to rehire an adjunct faculty member once the semester is over or discourage their continued employment by offering them fewer classes. . . . No cause need be provided, nor is any face-to-face discussion required for a non-renewal decision. The same circumstances that apply to a first-semester adjunct also apply to one with fifteen years of nearly continuous service. . . . It is hard to argue that adjunct faculty enjoy academic freedom when the risk of dissent or professional disagreement is loss of a job with no recourse to dispute resolution procedures."[23]

If the tenure system has at times *appeared*—and, more often than it should be, has actually *been*—elitist, the emerging "gig academy" offers anything but an egalitarian alternative. Contingent hiring must entail continuous monitoring and assessment of faculty work, too often by nonfaculty bureaucrats. The result is frequently a culture of, as Ernst Benjamin put it, either "mutual back-scratching or mutual back-stabbing." As a consequence, Michael Bérubé and Jennifer Ruth have argued that "hiring legions of faculty off the tenure track leads to the creation of fiefdoms and patronage systems." This is bad enough, but at too many institutions the new reality is a system governed neither by professionalism nor patronage but by managerial fiat.[24]

In this environment the shrinking minority of tenured and tenure-track faculty are cast in the role of props to a reconfigured and expanding unprofessional structure. The focus shifts from the faculty as a community of self-governing scholars to the faculty as a collection of individual struggling entrepreneurs. As a result, the increasing vulnerability of those outside the tenure system inevitably bleeds into that system itself. "Once dethroned, a costly and unruly tenured faculty will be hard pressed to secure its own restoration," adjuncts correctly warn.[25]

In the dark days of the anti-Communist hysteria of the 1950s, tenured faculty members were fired, often with little to no due process. But then, as today, that number was small compared with the hundreds whose appointments were contingent, of limited term, and quietly not renewed when their political beliefs came under suspicion. Hence, given the erosion of tenure, the academic profession as a whole is today more vulnerable to shifting political winds and the whims of academic fashion than it has been in some time.

Education writer John Warner has distinguished "tenure as principle" from "tenure as policy." The latter, he writes, "has become something to be doled out to the elect, and has allowed for the establishment of a multi-tiered faculty, where only the top tier has access to the protections of 'tenure as principle.'" It "has emerged gradually over time as a consequence of the corporatized university. It is not the fault of currently tenured faculty. Currently tenured faculty should also not feel any personal guilt over the establishment of this system over which they had no control." Warner advocates extending "the values of tenure to those who don't have access to them." But, he adds, that cannot be the responsibility solely of "contingent faculty who do not have the academic freedom or job security or economic standing of tenured faculty. . . . The sooner this is tackled by tenured faculty, the better. It will be better to figure this out while some faculty still have tenure and some of the power that goes with it, than to wait until it diminishes further or is wiped away entirely, and there is no reason for legislatures or administrations to listen or act on faculty desires, and suddenly all faculty know what it is to be contingent."[26]

If the movement toward a deprofessionalized precariat with stunted ability to defend academic freedom is to be arrested, the problem will need to be addressed in multiple ways. Of course, academic freedom and shared governance have always been aspirational, but aspirations can and have become realities. In the end the goal should be clear: if academic freedom is to survive as more than hollow promise and empty rhetoric, we must rebuild the system of tenure.

Chapter 6

Law

In 1819, the US Supreme Court ruled in *Trustees of Dartmouth College* v. *Woodward* that, although the college had not been founded for private gain but to benefit the public, it remained a private enterprise shielded from government intervention. The case is sometimes considered a landmark in the history of academic freedom because it protected private educational institutions from political meddling; but it also expanded the privileges of private enterprise against claims of the common good. Moreover, its logic ran counter to that advanced by the AAUP's founders almost a century later. They would deem all universities to be public trusts and built their arguments for professional autonomy and academic freedom on that basis. By contrast, "in rescuing private colleges from politicians," Louis Menand pointed out, "the Court effectively turned them over to the trustees. It did not turn them over to the professors."[1]

Academic freedom and freedom of speech were not at issue in *Dartmouth College,* but that decision's arrogation to external trustees of the power to control institutions of higher education would haunt the court's decisions when, in the twentieth century, the justices gradually and haltingly crafted an interpretation of the First Amendment that would come to encompass academic freedom. That interpretation was first signaled by Justice Oliver Wendell Holmes Jr.'s famous 1919 dissent in *Abrams v. United States*, which employed the now common metaphor of the "marketplace of ideas" to argue that a sedition law violated the First Amendment. Holmes's view gradually gained traction and emerged largely triumphant after World War II. But it would not be until 1952 that the words "academic freedom" first appeared in a Supreme Court opinion, and the concept would only come to be considered "a special concern of the First Amendment" in 1967.

In the late 1940s and 1950s, as part of the widespread anti-Communist panic of the period, many states adopted loyalty oaths, which required public employees to pledge not only their fealty to the US and state constitutions but to disavow affiliation with allegedly Communist organizations. The movement swept up hundreds of public college and university instructors, who either refused or failed to sign at the cost of their employment. Others were dismissed or not reappointed after they declined to testify before federal or state investigating committees. In these efforts, as Richard Hofstadter pointed out, "Communism was not the target but the weapon," deployed against liberalism and intellect more broadly.[2]

In its 1956 special report, *Academic Freedom and Tenure in the Quest for National Security*, the AAUP reviewed cases at eighteen colleges, universities, and university systems, including loyalty oath controversies in California, Washington, and New York. "Nothing in the record of college and university teachers as a group justifies the imputation to them of a tendency toward disloyalty to the government or toward subversive intent with respect to the nation's institutions," the report declared. On that basis it opposed "disclaimer oaths" as violations of academic freedom.[3] The Supreme Court, however, had already upheld such mandatory oaths as constitutional on the ground that teachers, because they work in a "sensitive area," involving the shaping

of minds, may be subject to investigation for their political affiliations and beliefs.

The Supreme Court from *Adler* to *Keyishian*

That ruling came in *Adler v. Board of Education,* decided in 1952. The
case unsuccessfully challenged New York's Feinberg Law, a
loyalty oath statute requiring investigations of the political associations of public school teachers. The decision is noteworthy,
however, for a dissenting opinion by Justice William O. Douglas, in which Justice Hugo Black concurred. Douglas argued that
the law would "raise havoc with academic freedom." Feinberg,
he said, "produces standardized thought, not the pursuit of
truth," whereby "a pall is cast over the classroom." As William
Van Alstyne noted, Douglas's dissent was not only the first use
by the court of the phrase "academic freedom," it also employed
the concept "as a distinct, identified subset of constitutional first
amendment concern" that is "not merely parasitic on a standard
free speech claim."[4]

Later that term, in *Wieman v. Updegraff,* the court overturned
an Oklahoma loyalty oath statute, albeit on extremely narrow
grounds. But Justice Felix Frankfurter's concurrence employed
logic similar to that used by Douglas in *Adler.* Calling teachers
"the priests of our democracy," Frankfurter bemoaned the oath's
"unwarranted inhibition upon the free spirit of teachers" and its
"unmistakable tendency to chill that free play of the spirit which
all teachers ought especially to cultivate and practice." The
job of teachers, he added, is "to foster those habits of open-
mindedness and critical inquiry which alone make for responsible citizens." Nevertheless, for the remainder of the decade the
court still upheld nearly every loyalty law that came before it.

In June 1957, the Supreme Court in a single day decided four
cases that together marked the first serious judicial challenge to
the repression of the era. Among these was the case of *Sweezy v.
New Hampshire*, which reversed the contempt conviction of a

scholar who had refused to answer questions posed by the state's attorney general.[5] The majority opinion by Chief Justice Earl Warren used language that powerfully appealed to academic freedom. "The essentiality of freedom in the community of American universities is almost self-evident," he wrote. "Scholarship cannot flourish in an atmosphere of suspicion and distrust. Teachers and students must always remain free to inquire, to study and to evaluate, to gain new maturity and understanding; otherwise, our civilization will stagnate and die." Nonetheless, Warren's ruling did not rest on these eloquent sentiments but on the narrower procedural ground of due process.

A concurring opinion by Frankfurter, joined by Justice John Harlan, would have decided the case explicitly on First Amendment academic freedom grounds, rather than on due process. But while Warren paid homage to the individual academic freedom of professors and students, Frankfurter would define the right of academic freedom in terms of universities' institutional autonomy. "This means the exclusion of governmental intervention in the intellectual life of a university. It matters little whether such intervention occurs avowedly or through action that inevitably tends to check the ardor and fearlessness of scholars." On these grounds, Frankfurter identified "four essential freedoms of a university—to determine for itself on academic grounds who may teach, what may be taught, how it shall be taught, and who may be admitted to study."[6] This definition of academic freedom as adhering to the institution would retain great influence, but it would often be forgotten that it sought to exclude government intervention only in "the *intellectual* life of the university" but not necessarily in other spheres, including, for example, labor relations and governance institutions.

In 1967, the court returned to New York's Feinberg Law, which it had upheld in the 1952 *Adler* ruling. This time five faculty members at the State University of New York challenged the statute. They lost in lower courts, which were bound to apply *Adler*. But in a 5-4 ruling, the Supreme Court overturned its precedent.

The majority opinion in *Keyishian v. Board of Regents*, written by Justice William J. Brennan Jr., placed the protection of academic freedom at the heart of the First Amendment. Its language would be quoted repeatedly by future courts:

> Our nation is deeply committed to safeguarding academic freedom, which is of transcendent value to all of us and not merely to the teachers concerned. That freedom is therefore a special concern of the First Amendment, which does not tolerate laws that cast a pall of orthodoxy over the classroom. . . . 'The vigilant protection of constitutional freedoms is nowhere more vital than in the community of American schools.' . . . The classroom is peculiarly the 'marketplace of ideas.' The Nation's future depends upon leaders trained through wide exposure to that robust exchange of ideas which discovers truth 'out of a multitude of tongues, (rather) than through any kind of authoritative selection.'"[7]

Faculty or Institutional Academic Freedom?

If a First Amendment commitment to the protection of academic freedom was now the law of the land, whose academic freedom would it protect? Was it the freedom of the professor—or, as the AAUP would have it, of the academic profession—to teach, conduct research, and speak as a citizen free of institutional constraint, as Warren's language in *Sweezy* might have suggested? Or was it defined by the institution's four freedoms from government intrusion celebrated in Frankfurter's concurrence, with its echoes of the 1819 *Dartmouth College* decision? Brennan's opinion offered no definition. Hence the jurisprudence of academic freedom has been characterized ever since by unresolved tensions about who the principle protects and in what ways. Most cases involving academic freedom in the 1950s and 1960s "focused on faculty and institutional freedom from external (political) intrusion," two scholars have explained. "These cases pitted the faculty and institution against the State. Since the early 1970s, however, academic freedom cases have focused primarily on faculty freedom from institutional intrusion. In these latter cases, faculty academic freedom has collided with institutional academic freedom."[8]

The record of the courts in providing First Amendment protection for the faculty's academic freedom, as defined by the 1940 *Statement*, is spotty at best, even with respect to public institutions. At the Supreme Court, few cases unambiguously do so. In 1968, the court decided the case of *Epperson v. Arkansas*, a reprise on the infamous *Scopes* case of the 1920s. An Arkansas law that forbade any teacher at any level, including the university, to assign a textbook espousing the Darwinian theory of evolution was challenged by a high school biology teacher. At the Supreme Court, Justice Abe Fortas appealed to academic freedom, invoking *Keyishian*, but in the end his opinion, and the court's decision, struck down the law on grounds of the First Amendment's Establishment Clause. More troubling was this passage in Justice Black's concurring opinion: "I am . . . not ready to hold that a person hired to teach school children takes with him into the classroom a constitutional right to teach sociological, economic, political, or religious subjects that the school's managers do not want discussed. . . . I question whether it is absolutely certain, as the Court's opinion indicates, that 'academic freedom' permits a teacher to breach his contractual agreement to teach only the subjects designated by the school authorities who hired him."[9] While this view might have been defensible when applied to elementary and even secondary schools, its implications for higher education were alarming.

In the 1972 case of *Board of Regents v. Roth*, a faculty member at the University of Wisconsin–Oshkosh charged that he had been dismissed from his probationary position without explanation but actually in retaliation for his public criticism of the campus administration. A district court judge held that the professor's status as a tenure-track appointee distinguished him from other contract faculty such that he was entitled to some sort of intramural due process procedure before he could be terminated. The university appealed. The AAUP filed an amicus brief in the case, which argued, first, that any peremptory power not to renew a faculty member's appointment without explanation threatened academic freedom. It also argued that a tenure-track appointment implies a more ongoing relationship than other term appointments, even if it doesn't offer the extent of protection provided by tenure, and hence required greater due process protection. Justice Douglas agreed, as did Justices Brennan and Thurgood Marshall. The majority, however, disagreed and reversed the ruling of the district court.[10]

As Van Alstyne pointed out, "the majority in *Roth* cast no retrospective doubt" on previous rulings that had protected academic freedom under the First Amendment. They also left little doubt that "insofar as [the professor's] nonrenewal was improperly based . . . he could prevail in his action, once he proved his claim. But the Court detached that means of protecting his academic freedom—by suing and by proving affirmatively in court the improper basis of the regents' action—from the claim that his tenure track status entitled him to something more from the university than an unexplained pink slip, if academic freedom was not to be put unfairly at risk."[11]

Some lower courts have ruled that faculty members at public institutions may not be dismissed based on their political views. In *Cooper v. Ross*, a 1979 case involving an untenured history professor at the University of Arkansas not rehired because he was a member of the Communist Party, the district court concluded that "at least in the context of a university classroom" professors have "a constitutionally protected right to inform students" of their "personal political and philosophical views" but not "to proselytize students or to devote so much class time to such matters that . . . coverage of the prescribed subject matter is impaired." In the 1983 case of *Ollman v. Toll*, a Maryland court rejected political scientist Bertell Ollman's claim that he had been turned down for the position of department chair because of his Marxist views. The court determined he had failed to demonstrate that this was the principal motivating factor in the decision. Still, the court acknowledged that "no more direct assault on academic freedom can be imagined than for school authorities to refuse to hire a teacher because of his or her political, philosophical, or ideological beliefs."[12]

If the Supreme Court has failed clearly to define the scope of First Amendment academic freedom's protection for individual faculty members, it has been somewhat more expansive about the scope of institutional protection. In the 1978 case of *Regents of the University of California v. Bakke* and subsequent affirmative action cases, the court has relied on the doctrine of institutional autonomy implicit in Frankfurter's *Sweezy* concurrence. The controlling opinion in *Bakke* was signed by Justice Lewis Powell and joined by no other member of the court. Van Alstyne called it "one of the most well-disposed treatments of 'academic freedom' one can find" among the court's cases. Matthew Finkin, however, argued that to apply the term *academic freedom* to institutional autonomy unrelated to the maintenance of conditions of the faculty's professional academic freedom is "particularly perverse." On Powell's opinion in *Bakke*, Finkin wrote, "Inasmuch as no nexus between the exercise of academic freedom and the claim of institutional autonomy need be shown, the interests insulated are not necessarily those of teachers and researchers, but administration and the governing board; the effect is to insulate managerial decisionmaking from close scrutiny, even in cases where the rights or interests of the faculty might be adverse to the institution's administration."[13]

Insofar as jurisprudence has privileged institutional autonomy, it has often been based on an idealized assumption that the faculty wields appropriate authority over curriculum and academic standards in the institution. In *Regents of the University of Michigan v. Ewing*, Justice John Paul Stevens, writing for a unanimous court, declared, "Academic freedom thrives not only on the independent and uninhibited exchange of ideas among teachers and students . . . but *also*, and somewhat inconsistently, on autonomous decision making by the academy itself. . . . When judges are asked to review the substance of a genuinely academic decision . . . they may not override it unless it is such a substantial departure from accepted academic norms as to demonstrate that the person or committee responsible did not actually exercise professional judgment."[14]

How, one might ask, can a court determine whether a decision is "genuinely academic"? Legal scholar J. Peter Byrne has argued that "the term 'academic freedom' should be reserved for those rights necessary for the preservation of the unique functions of the university, particularly the goals of disinterested scholarship and teaching." He therefore recommended that "universities that do not respect the academic freedom of professors . . . ought not to be afforded institutional autonomy."[15]

It is by no means clear that the courts have or will yet adopt such a principle, however, or that they will acknowledge the many ways in which structures of university governance have grown more authoritarian and the faculty's influence diluted since the 1960s. Byrne's principle might well be expanded to encompass institutions where the faculty's role in governance, particularly on matters of curriculum, teaching and academic standards, is not appropriately respected. In 2000, the US Court of Appeals for the Fourth Circuit, ruling 8-4 *en banc* in the case of *Urofsky v. Gilmore*, declared that "any right of 'academic freedom' . . . inheres in the University, not in individual professors," adding, not entirely correctly, that the Supreme Court "has focused discussions of academic freedom solely on issues of institutional autonomy." The court majority asserted that academic freedom for professors is essentially a professional norm, not a constitutional right. In a foreshadowing of the Supreme Court's 2006 ruling in *Garcetti v. Ceballos* (see below), the court declared, with respect to the speech of public employees, including professors, that "the government is entitled to control the content of the speech because it has, in a meaningful sense, 'purchased' the speech at issue through a grant of funding or payment of salary." An appeal to the Supreme Court was denied.[16]

The court's view in *Urofsky v. Gilmore* was echoed in 2018 by attorneys representing the University of Texas in a suit brought by professors, who argued that a campus "open carry" gun law violated their academic freedom. The university's attorneys told the court that "academic freedom, if it exists, belongs to the institution, not the individual professor." The university's faculty was appalled, and the president quickly reassured them that system policies guaranteed freedom in research and teaching. But the attorneys retorted that this was "a workplace policy," not a protection provided by the First Amendment.[17] That opinion was not unfounded, given the continuing confusion in the precedents between institutional and faculty academic freedom.

Representation and Faculty Unions

In *Minnesota State Board for Community Colleges v. Knight,* several nonunion faculty members challenged a state law that, on the one hand, obligated the state board governing the community colleges to "meet and confer" with faculty on matters of educational policy, but, on the other hand, forbade the board from permitting any faculty member to attend such meetings unless designated by whatever union had won exclusive collective bargaining rights, even if these were not bargaining sessions and meant to address other issues. The district court held that this restricted the First Amendment academic freedom of nonunion faculty. The Supreme Court reversed.

Justice Sandra Day O'Connor wrote for the court over a dissent by Justice Brennan, joined by Justices Powell and Stevens, and a partial dissent by Justice Marshall. The majority saw the case as a matter of meetings that needn't have been scheduled but still offered an opportunity for substantial faculty representation, even if that was limited to designees of the faculty's union.

O'Connor acknowledged that "there is a strong, if not universal or uniform, tradition of faculty participation in school governance, and there are numerous policy arguments to support such participation." However, she added rather ominously for First Amendment faculty academic freedom, "even assuming that speech rights guaranteed by the First Amendment take on a special meaning in an academic setting . . . there is no constitutional right to participate in academic governance."

In dissent Justice Brennan responded,

> freedom to explore novel or controversial ideas in the classroom is closely linked to the freedom of faculty members to express their views to the administration concerning matters of academic governance. . . . The freedom to teach without inhibition may be jeopardized just as gravely by a restriction on the faculty's ability to speak out on such matters as by the more direct restrictions struck down in *Keyishian* and in *Epperson*. In my view, therefore, a direct prohibition of some identified faculty group from submitting their views concerning academic policy questions for consideration by college administrators would plainly violate the principles of academic freedom enshrined in the First Amendment.[18]

Insofar as the Minnesota faculty union emerged victorious in the case, *Knight* marked a victory for collective bargaining. But O'Connor's argument hardly embraced faculty interests, instead implicitly supporting institutional prerogative. The court's decision four years earlier in *National Labor Relations Board v. Yeshiva University*, though not a First Amendment case, had also been based on the doctrine of institutional autonomy and marked a significant defeat for both unionism and academic freedom. In *Yeshiva*, the court overturned a decision by the NLRB that allowed faculty to unionize, ruling instead that those on the tenure track are "managerial employees" and thus ineligible to organize a union under the board's protection. The decision has since prevented the overwhelming majority of tenured and tenure-track faculty members at private institutions from unionizing. As law professor Robert Gorman wrote, "several members of the Court were beguiled by the medieval maxim that the faculty *is* the university. The Court majority gave conclusive weight to the influence of the Yeshiva faculty upon university decisions regarding personnel and educational policy. It rejected the arguments . . . that faculty decisions are generally endorsed by the administration not because the faculty are 'managers' but rather because of the faculty's special competence as 'professional employees' (who are covered by the National Labor Relations Act)."[19]

In a sense *Yeshiva* continued the line of reasoning commencing with *Dartmouth College* and reflected in the doctrine of institutional academic freedom derived from Frankfurter's *Sweezy* concurrence, which treats the trustees and managers responsible to them, not the faculty, as the university's masters. The majority opinion, delivered by Justice Powell, argued that principles developed for use in the industrial setting cannot be "imposed blindly on the academic world." In dissent, Justice Brennan, joined by Justices White, Marshall, and Blackmun, responded, "The Court purports to recognize that there are fundamental differences between the authority structures of the typical industrial and academic institutions which preclude the blind transplanting of principles developed in one arena onto the other; yet it nevertheless ignores those very differences in concluding that Yeshiva's faculty is excluded from the Act's coverage."

Brennan continued,

the Board determined that the faculty at Yeshiva exercised its decisionmaking authority in its own interest rather than "in the interest of the employer." The Court, in contrast, can perceive "no justification for this distinction" and concludes that the faculty's interests "cannot be separated from those of the institution." But the Court's vision is clouded by its failure fully to discern and comprehend the nature of the faculty's role in university governance.

Unlike the purely hierarchical decisionmaking structure that prevails in the typical industrial organization, the bureaucratic foundation of most "mature" universities is characterized by dual authority systems. The primary decisional network is hierarchical in nature: Authority is lodged in the administration, and a formal chain of command runs from a lay governing board down through university officers to individual faculty members and students. At the same time, there exists a parallel professional network, in which formal mechanisms have been created to bring the expertise of the faculty into the decisionmaking process.

What the Board realized—and what the Court fails to apprehend—is that whatever influence the faculty wields in university decisionmaking is attributable solely to its collective expertise as professional educators, and not to any managerial or supervisory prerogatives.

Brennan's opinion usefully described the distinction between managerial authority and the governance responsibilities of the faculty. Unfortunately, that distinction was not accepted by the majority, nor has it been reflected in subsequent federal and state court decisions.

The troubling conclusion to be drawn from the court's decisions in *Knight* and *Yeshiva* is that if the faculty's speech on university affairs may be restricted by legislation authorizing union representation (*Knight*), the faculty may also be denied a union voice for that expression (*Yeshiva*). In these decisions, the implications of the judicial doctrine of institutional academic freedom seriously undermined judicial support for the independent professional academic freedom of the faculty within the institution.

From *Pickering* to *Janus*

Insofar as the judiciary has recognized the professional academic freedom of the faculty, the focus has been on teaching and research. But academic freedom also protects faculty members' expression as officers of their institutions and as citizens. As previously noted, this is precisely where, in practice, the protections of professional academic freedom most resemble those provided by the First Amendment. The First Amendment protects only against unwarranted speech restrictions by government, not private institutions, where protection for the faculty's extramural expression must be established by institutional policies based on the principles of academic freedom. At public colleges and universities, however, it seems reasonable that faculty expression might also be protected by the Constitution.

As public employees, do faculty members at state colleges and universities enjoy First Amendment protections for their speech as citizens? That is a question the Supreme Court addressed indirectly in 1968 in *Pickering v. Board of Education*. Marvin Pickering, an Illinois public high-school teacher, was dismissed after he had published a letter critical of his school board's budget priorities. The Illinois Supreme Court affirmed his dismissal. Overturning that decision, the US Supreme Court formulated a balancing test, weighing "the interests of the teacher, as a citizen, in commenting upon matters of public concern" against "the interest of the State, as an employer, in promoting the efficiency of the public services it performs through its employees."[20] As a 2009 AAUP report would later point out, in establishing the "matter of public concern" test, "the Court's thrust may have been to protect a public employee's speech as a citizen rather than as a government worker."[21] However, more ominously and in retrospect "clearly portentous" was the possibility "that the justices were from the outset committed only to protecting public employees when they spoke . . . on matters remote from their field of expertise or assigned responsibility." What constitutes a matter of public concern? The difference between a matter of public concern and a matter of private interest, two commentators point out, can be "difficult to draw in many contexts, but is perhaps especially so in the context of classroom speech," rendering the application of *Pickering* to academic freedom problematic.[22] Nonetheless, the AAUP report concluded, "the judicial development and refinement of the *Pickering* doctrine . . . had remarkably limited import for faculty speech or for academic freedom."

Until 2006, that is, and the Supreme Court's decision in *Garcetti v. Ceballos.* The case involved an assistant district attorney who had reported fraud to his superiors and testified about that at a hearing. He sued after he was passed over for promotion and punitively transferred. In denying his claim, a narrow five-member majority, in an opinion written by Justice Anthony Kennedy, implicitly called into question whether it would still recognize a First Amendment right to individual academic freedom for public college and university faculty as articulated in *Keyishian.* The ruling declared that "when public employees make statements pursuant to their official duties, the employees are not speaking as citizens for First Amendment purposes, and the Constitution does not insulate their communications from employer discipline." While not overturning *Pickering, Garcetti* established a new "official duties" test, which would in effect be applied prior to the "public concern" test.[23]

The implications for academic freedom were stark. Not only did faculty intramural expression—say, while participating in committees or in an academic senate, all "official duties"—stand to lose protection. Teaching and scholarship are also among a professor's "official duties." It was possible that under a strict application of the *Garcetti* test, public college and university faculty members could enjoy First Amendment protections only for statements they might make on topics wholly outside their professional research and teaching expertise and their institutional roles.

In dissent, Justice David Souter recognized this problem, expressing alarm at the decision's creation of an "ostensible domain beyond the pale of the First Amendment [that] is spacious enough to include even the teaching of a public university professor." Joined by Justices Stevens and Ruth Bader Ginsburg, he warned that the decision could "imperil First Amendment academic freedom in public colleges and universities, whose teachers necessarily speak and write pursuant to 'official duties.'" In response, Justice Kennedy offered an ambiguous reservation: "We need not, and for that reason do not, decide whether the analysis we conduct today would apply in the same manner to a case involving speech related to scholarship and teaching," leaving unmentioned, however, speech exercised in the course of college and university governance activities.

The extent of *Garcetti*'s impact on academic freedom remains unclear, as the court has not returned to the issue. Lower courts, however, have seemed eager to apply the ruling to professorial expression. A California district court rejected claims by a tenured engineering professor who had criticized administrative practices in his school and was subsequently denied a merit salary increase on the grounds that "a faculty member's official duties are not limited to classroom instruction and professional research" but also "include a wide range of academic, administrative, and personnel functions." The court concluded that the university "is entitled to unfettered discretion when it restricts statements an employee makes on the job and according to his professional responsibilities."[24] The US Court of Appeals for the Seventh Circuit held that administration of research grants was part of a University of Wisconsin–Milwaukee professor's official duties and dismissed a First Amendment retaliation claim. An Arkansas court held that a tenured professor, dismissed after nineteen years of service, could not claim retaliation for an email complaint because it expressed her "dissatisfaction with an internal employment policy." A Mississippi court ruled that speech between a professor and a student constituted classroom speech made in an official capacity and hence was not subject to First Amendment protection. In Alabama, a court applied *Garcetti* to a case involving an assistant professor who alleged she was dismissed because she had raised the issue of diversity during department meetings, attendance at which was part of her "official duties."[25]

On the other hand, two US appellate circuits have ruled that *Garcetti* should not be applied in the university setting. In 2011, the Fourth Circuit found that speech provided to a tenure review committee should be insulated from the *Garcetti* test by virtue of Justice Kennedy's reservation about its application to issues of "academic scholarship or classroom instruction." In 2014, the Ninth Circuit ruled in a case involving a tenured professor who charged retaliation after he distributed some of his writings, that *Garcetti* "does not apply to speech related to scholarship or teaching." The case was, the court opined, precisely "the kind of case that worried Justice Souter." Because "teaching and academic writing are at the core of the official duties of teachers and professors," the opinion continued, they "are 'a special concern of the First Amendment.' We conclude that if applied to teaching and academic writing, *Garcetti* would directly conflict with the important First Amendment values previously articulated by the Supreme Court."[26]

In 2018, by a 5-4 vote, the Supreme Court in *Janus v. AFSCME Council 31* overturned a unanimous 1977 decision, declaring that in the public sector compulsory payments to unions by nonunion members for the costs of representation violate the First Amendment. The decision was a blow to faculty unions, although as it turned out, not as severe as many unions had feared and union opponents had hoped. Justice Kennedy, author of the *Garcetti* ruling, joined the majority even though the logic of Justice Samuel Alito's majority opinion ran against the thrust of both *Pickering* and *Garcetti*. In an amicus brief, Charles Fried, professor of law at Harvard and US solicitor general under President Reagan, and Robert Post argued that

> public-sector bargaining regimes involve the same state managerial prerogatives to which the Court has expressed deference in the *Garcetti* line of cases. . . . This Court has interpreted the First

Amendment, consistent with *Garcetti*, to give ample room to state employers to structure public workplaces as they believed most effective, without undue First Amendment restrictions. . . . It is inconsistent with *Garcetti*'s carefully drawn distinction between speaking as an employee and speaking as a citizen to hold that the compulsory payment of agency fees is categorically protected under the First Amendment. Any such holding would therefore threaten to transform every workplace dispute into a constitutional controversy. . . . If the employee speech at issue here can be restricted or compelled without First Amendment challenge, so too can the funding of such speech.

The record shows that the kinds of activities funded by these fees, the brief continued, "cover the very types of routine workplace matters that the Court has carefully refrained from constitutionalizing with First Amendment protections. . . . A ruling categorically prohibiting agency fees would necessarily elevate these types of pedestrian workplace matters into matters of public concern. . . . If the Court in this case holds that employee grievances are a matter of public concern, it will have to accept the same result in countless other scenarios."[27]

Contract Law

Until July 6, 2018, no US court had explicitly affirmed the AAUP's position on extramural speech. On that date, however, the Supreme Court of Wisconsin ruled 4-2 in favor of Marquette University professor John McAdams, who had sued for reinstatement after he was suspended for comments made on his blog. The decision in *McAdams v. Marquette* was founded not on the First Amendment but on the terms of the professor's contract, which incorporated the university's policy commitment to protect academic freedom, with the court explicitly stating that it "does not rely upon the United States Constitution for any part of its decision." The ruling had problematic elements, and cynical observers have argued that the Republican majority found for McAdams more out of sympathy with his views opposing gay marriage than support for his academic freedom to express them. Nonetheless, the decision marked a powerful, and relatively rare, judicial endorsement of AAUP principles, especially the AAUP's understanding of academic freedom in extramural expression:

> The analytical structure described by the AAUP . . . provides a stable framework within which to evaluate whether the doctrine of academic freedom protects a specific extramural comment. Although the doctrine may not be susceptible to precise definition, still it is sufficiently certain that it can inform faculty members what is required of them. The AAUP properly limits the analysis to whether the actual extramural comment, on its face, clearly demonstrates that the professor is unfit to serve. This very narrow inquiry explains why the AAUP can confidently state that "extramural utterances rarely bear upon the faculty member's fitness for the position."

The decision overturned not only the university's actions but also the recommendations of a duly constituted faculty committee, which had found that not all of McAdams's actions were protected by academic freedom. In response the dissenters appealed to "the academic freedom of the institution," to which the majority opinion caustically responded that a "university's academic freedom is a shield against governmental interference; the dissent, however, would reforge it as a sword with which to strike down contracts it no longer wishes to honor."[28]

The *McAdams* case provides support for legal scholar Philip Lee's contention that "while constitutional law is still the proper mechanism for defending institutional rights from government interference, contract law should be the primary mechanism for protecting professorial academic freedom."[29] In 1990, Ralph Brown and Jordan Kurland considered it "still uncertain" how the Supreme Court might handle "a straightforward case in which an untenured professor has been disciplined for the content of classroom utterances or scholarly writing." They expressed optimism, nonetheless, that "direct resort to the first amendment in support of claims of denial of academic freedom has a brightening future." They even imagined "a transformation of our legal system so that it would offer comprehensive relief for persons deprived of their academic freedom."[30] Today, after *Garcetti* and in the absence of decisions extending support for the faculty's professional academic freedom since *Keyishian*, such hopes unfortunately seem far-fetched.

If the academic freedom of professors—as opposed to that of the institutions that employ them—is to find strong support, it is now likely to come less from First Amendment law and more from common law tradition and contractual protections designed to strengthen the faculty's role. In a 1969 case, *Greene v. Howard University*, Judge Carl McGowan of the District of Columbia Circuit ruled that faculty employment contracts may be read to include within their scope institutional commitments to academic freedom contained in faculty handbooks and similar policy documents. "Contracts are written, and are to be read," McGowan wrote, "by reference to the norms of conduct and expectations founded upon them. This is especially true of contracts in and among a community of scholars, which is what a university is." In this view, written policies and customary practices as incorporated in faculty handbooks may be interpreted by courts in the context of what a later court deemed the "unwritten 'common law' in a particular university."[31]

Still, faculty handbooks and even collective bargaining agreements may have varying degrees of legal enforceability. Beginning in the 1980s, when some workers began asserting that provisions in their companies' employee manuals were contractually binding, courts allowed employers to disclaim such status. That position was then sometimes applied to similar college and university policy documents. The AAUP today informs its members that "contract claims are primarily based on state law, and the law affecting the claims varies greatly from state to state. A majority of states have held that contractual terms can at times be implied from communications such as oral assurances, pre-employment statements, or handbooks. Of these, faculty hand-books are the most common source of implied contract terms."[32] The inclusion in legally enforceable faculty contracts, in collective bargaining agreements, and in university policy manuals of provisions and regulations designed to support both academic freedom and tenure can thus protect faculty in both private and public institutions. Where possible, however, faculty handbooks and collective agreements should explicitly provide that policies protecting academic freedom be contractually binding and that courts should take them as such.

Academic freedom in the United States can claim limited, at best, legal standing. It "floats in the law," one scholar quipped, "picking up decisions as a hull does barnacles."[33] As former AAUP Senior Counsel Rachel Levinson-Waldman has written, the AAUP over the years "built a multilayered 'common law' of academic freedom . . . considered by many academics to be the ultimate arbiter on the matter." That common law can provide the basis not only for contract language but also for the enforcement of professional standards by means of moral suasion and political pressure. By contrast, the approach of the judiciary "has generally been a series of gut feelings in search of a coherent philosophy."[34]

Chapter 7

Students

The 1915 *Declaration* acknowledged that "academic freedom has traditionally had two applications: to the freedom of the teacher and to that of the student, *Lehrfreiheit* [to teach] and *Lernfreiheit* [to learn]." In 1929, the AAUP investigated a case in which members of a student group were disciplined for "insubordination" after they invited a controversial speaker to campus. The investigation concluded that the association "cannot concern itself in a case of student discipline as such, even though such discipline may be unjust and excessive," adding that the university's discretion to punish "is not subject to review on the ground of academic freedom," although the faculty should be consulted in such matters. Nonetheless, "so long as a group of students speaks in its own name, we believe that it ought to be unmolested in its expression of opinion on public questions," the report added. "Any other position implies an intolerable censorship of all student opinion by the administration." In 1956, AAUP general secretary Ralph Fuchs called student freedom "a traditional accompaniment to faculty freedom as an element of academic freedom in the larger sense."[1] It would not be until the 1960s, however, that the American academic community, including the AAUP, seriously turned its attention to considering the academic freedom and free speech rights of students.

Walter Metzger has summarized the German understanding of *Lernfreiheit* cited in the 1915 *Declaration*:

> Literally, *Lernfreiheit* meant "learning freedom" and in a bare decoding could signify no more than the absence of required courses. In Germany, it meant much more than that: it amounted to a disclaimer by the university of any control over the students' course of study save that which they needed to prepare them for state professional examinations or to qualify them for an academic teaching license. It also absolved the university of any responsibility for students' private conduct, provided they kept the peace and paid their bills. . . . The German university confronted its student body primarily as a purveyor of knowledge and as a credentializing agency, not as a parent surrogate or landlord. For their part, German students, obliged to find their own lodgings and diversions, liberated from course grades and classroom roll calls, free to move from place to place sampling academic wares, presented themselves to the university as mature and self-reliant beings, not as neophytes, tenants, or wards.[2]

If American scholars eagerly adapted principles of *Lehrfreiheit* in developing their theory of faculty academic freedom, the vision summarized by Metzger stood as a polar opposite to the doctrine of *in loco parentis*, accepted largely without faculty objection by most US colleges and universities, especially residential and private institutions, until the 1960s. *In loco parentis* was derived from English Common Law and the notion that schools had not only educational but also moral responsibility for students. Well into the twentieth century, courts gave broad authority to schools and colleges to regulate and discipline student behavior, repeatedly rebuffing claims by student plaintiffs. Under *in loco parentis*, undergraduates confronted an array of restrictions on their private lives. Women were generally subject to curfews. Dormitories were sex-segregated, with so-called parietal hours—

when students could entertain visitors of the opposite sex—which were severely limited and strictly enforced. Some universities expelled students, especially female students deemed "morally" undesirable. As late as 1968, Barnard College, in New York, whose policies were less restrictive than many, sought to expel a student for living off-campus with her boyfriend. More important, in conjunction with such restrictions, universities often also limited freedom of student speech, banning organizations out of favor or with controversial views from speaking, organizing, or demonstrating on campus.

Student Protests

Such restrictions had been eroding for decades, especially on urban commuter campuses, where radical political activism could be extensive, as at City College of New York in the 1930s.[3] But a broader assault on the doctrine dates from the mid-1950s, when Black student civil rights activists in the South first pushed against the barriers of both segregation and campus restrictions. As Joy Ann Williamson-Lott writes, "Student activists and their allies demanded that they enjoy all the rights and privileges guaranteed to American citizens and argued that they needed no *in loco parentis* practices to shield them."[4]

Northern white students who joined the civil rights struggle during 1964's Mississippi Summer brought that attitude with them when they returned to campus in the fall. At Berkeley they sought to organize support on campus for local civil rights activities—including illegal sit-ins—and in so doing ran into university restrictions on student political activity, much of it a legacy of the repressive anti-Communism of the preceding decade. The resulting Free Speech Movement (FSM) would have dramatic consequences for all of American higher education.

The victory of the FSM established, in the words of Erwin Chemerinsky and Howard Gilman, that "campuses should be open spaces, including for the noncivilized and nonscholarly expression of ideas." They add that "the AAUP approach to academic freedom was inextricably linked to professional standards and decorum; the FSM idea was not." However, according to Reginald Zelnik's authoritative account, the national AAUP supported those "liberal professors with a strong commitment to free speech and civil liberties" who worked to win support for the movement, many of whom were AAUP members. If the AAUP was concerned mainly with the academic freedom of the faculty, the FSM was concerned with the free expression rights of students. Yet its victory came only after the faculty had approved a resolution declaring that "the content of speech or advocacy should not be restricted by the University. Off-campus student political activities shall not be subject to University regulation. On-campus advocacy or organization of such activities shall be subject" only to limitations of time, place, and manner.[5]

The FSM was the first of the great student rebellions of the 1960s, and in many respects the most influential. Often treated as an episode in the rise of an increasingly radical and intolerant New Left, it was, at least in its demands, if not its tactics, an essentially liberal movement. As historian Robert Cohen has pointed out, "The campus restrictions on free speech that initially sparked mass activism at Berkeley offended not only students affiliated with the left but those in the center and on the right and even those with no political affiliation at all."[6]

In the aftermath of the FSM, student activism exploded on campuses across the country, culminating in the building occupations and strikes of 1968/70. Because so much of the unrest was directed against the escalating war in Southeast Asia, it is easy to forget that not only was the FSM prompted by the Black struggle for civil rights, but much of the subsequent turmoil had demands for diversity and minority rights at its core. At Columbia, San Francisco State, Berkeley, and Cornell, for examples, Black students led broader coalitions demanding more minority faculty and students and the institution of programs like Black Studies, directed toward their needs.[7]

After the deadly state violence directed in 1970 at protesters at Jackson State and Kent State universities, and the campus strikes that followed, the Nixon administration established a special commission on campus unrest. "The crisis on American campuses has no parallel in the history of our nation," the commission declared. Its report ostensibly affirmed many of the student protesters' concerns, all but demolishing *in loco parentis* in the process: "The goals, values, administration, and curriculum of the modern university have been sharply criticized by many students. Students complain that their studies are irrelevant to the social problems that concern them. They want to shape their own personal and common lives but find the university restrictive. They seek a community of companions and scholars, but find an impersonal multiversity." These demands could be viewed as potentially in conflict with the faculty's academic freedom to define curriculum, but that was hardly the commission's concern. After conceding some student grievances, the report quickly shifted to a critique of the protests themselves, decrying "a growing lack of tolerance, a growing insistence that their own views must govern, and impatience with the slow procedures of liberal democracy, a growing denial of the humanity and good will of those who urge patience and restraint, and particularly of those whose duty is to enforce the law."

As Roderick Ferguson has argued, "student demands were not seen as critiques of the social order and calls for social transformation but were instead often viewed as by-products of the students' irrationality." Such irrationality, many college and university administrators soon concluded, could be handled best by concessions to students' calls for personal, if not political, autonomy. In response to the unrest and to the emerging women's liberation movement, the late 1960s and early 1970s therefore saw an end to parietal hours and close supervision of campus social life. Coed dormitories, just a few years earlier seen as a utopian (or, for some, dystopian) ideal, now became commonplace, and many previously male- or female-only schools opened their doors to the opposite sex.[8]

The Courts Respond

Even before the FSM, courts had moved cautiously in the direction of expanding student rights. In 1961, the US Court of Appeals for the Fifth Circuit ruled in the landmark case *Dixon v. Alabama State Board of Education*, extending due process rights to students at tax-supported colleges. The case arose when Alabama State College, a then-segregated Black college, expelled six students without a hearing for unspecified reasons, but presumably because of their participation in demonstrations for civil rights. The case was appealed to the Fifth Circuit, which determined that in public institutions the due process clause of the US Constitution "requires notice and some opportunity for hearing" before students can be expelled for misconduct.[9]

In 1964, the Supreme Court heard a case brought by members of the faculty, staff, and student body at the University of Washington who sought relief from a state law requiring teachers to affirm by oath that they would "promote respect for the flag and institutions of [the United States and Washington] State." A remarkable feature of the case, *Baggett v. Bullitt*, was the court's acceptance of the student plaintiffs' standing to bring it. They had claimed separate standing because, they alleged, the law would have a direct impact on their academic freedom. As Van Alstyne commented, "the student academic freedom claim . . . is not in tension with the claim of academic freedom, advanced in the same case by the affected faculty. Rather, the two are exactly consistent in seeking an educational environment in which the good faith critical professional skills of the faculty are not foreclosed by hostile state action from being available to the students."[10] The student's freedom to learn and the faculty's freedom to teach were here seen as complementary.

On student free expression, the Supreme Court's 1969 decision in *Tinker v. Des Moines School District*, which famously declared that neither "students or teachers shed their constitutional rights to freedom of speech or expression at the schoolhouse gate," was a landmark. The 7-2 ruling held that three public school students (sixteen, fifteen, and thirteen years old) could not be penalized for defying a rule that forbade wearing armbands on campus in an antiwar protest. Although Justice Fortas claimed that this had been "the unmistakable holding of this Court for almost 50 years," in fact, as Van Alstyne noted, "no previous case had gone so far." Moreover, it is difficult to imagine the ruling had it not been for prior civil rights agitation and the victory of the FSM.[11]

Four years after *Tinker*, the court heard a First Amendment claim by college students in *Healy v. James*. A chapter of the Students for a Democratic Society had applied in 1969 for official recognition at Central Connecticut State College in order to qualify for the right to post notices and hold meetings on campus. Although other political groups had been recognized, the college president overruled a faculty-student committee and denied the request. He claimed that SDS "openly repudiates" the campus's commitment to academic freedom because chapters of the group elsewhere had been involved in disruptions. Lower courts supported him, but the Supreme Court unanimously reversed, in an opinion by Justice Powell.

In his opinion, Powell quoted *Tinker* and declared that "state colleges and universities are not enclaves immune from the sweep of the First Amendment." Even if SDS advocated violence and disruption, that "affords no reason" to disqualify it from recognition. "Whether petitioners did in fact advocate a philosophy of 'destruction' [is] immaterial," he wrote. "The College, acting here as the instrumentality of the State, may not restrict speech or association simply because it finds the views expressed by any group to be abhorrent."[12]

Unlike *Baggett,* neither *Tinker* nor *Healy* directly involved student academic freedom in the classroom, but their protections for student free speech, as Van Alstyne has argued, did "assure students of some right to fashion what is in some loose sense a constitutionally protected cocurriculum on campus—the teaching agendas and learning experiences of their own actions—carried on in a manner that may well influence the official curriculum as well."[13]

As Walter Metzger acknowledged, "students fit less snugly than teachers into the constitutional history of academic freedom." Nevertheless, "in the end, it seems best to conclude that, in the academic freedom club, students qualify as special members . . . because to keep them out would be anomalous and impoverishing."[14]

The Faculty Responds

In a concurring opinion in *Healy* Justice Douglas took dyspeptic aim at the faculty as a potential enemy of student freedoms. He wrote: "Some [of the faculty] have narrow specialties that are hardly relevant to modern times. History has passed others by, leaving them interesting relics of a bygone day. More often than not they represent those who withered under the pressures of McCarthyism or other forces of conformity and represent but a timid replica of those who once brought distinction to the ideal of academic freedom."

Douglas's jaundiced view was not, however, confirmed by the faculty's actions. In 1968, the AAUP appointed a special committee on "challenge and change" to study implications of the student rebellion. A year later it reported that "the turmoil we are witnessing would not exist if there were not . . . 'a shared sense that the nation has no plans for meeting the crises of our society.'" The report acknowledged that "students have come to be sharply critical of many features of the processes and institutions of higher education." It noted that students "object to their traditionally passive role in the educational process. . . . They resent being subject to rules and regulations which are, for the most part, not of their own making. Although, at many institutions, the process of government has been liberalized to provide for an active student role, there is nonetheless a basic validity to these complaints." After summarizing a series of specific student grievances, the report concluded, "We must guard ourselves against the traditional inertial failure to respond, which plagues most large institutions. . . . American colleges and universities must look for an improved way of meeting their major responsibilities to the students and to the American public."[15]

Individual faculty members had differing responses to campus unrest. These could highlight potential tensions, if not conflict, between the radical critique of the university offered by many protesting students and some faculty supporters and the faculty's historical claims under principles of academic freedom. Especially in the classroom, there is "tension between the necessary freedom of faculty to express their political perspectives, and the essential freedom of students to express differing views."[16] In 1970, the AAUP published several responses that illustrate these tensions.

The response by political theorist Alan Wolfe clearly resonates in the present decade. According to Wolfe,

> Many people feel that a university best serves its purposes when it is not being "politicized," that is, when the search for truth is not impeded by political considerations. Strange as it may sound to some, I agree fully with that proposition; what is arguable is the best way to achieve that goal. We must begin with the realization that in America the search for truth is constantly impeded by political considerations. . . . The American political system is characterized by vast areas of irrationality, expressed best in its wars, its domestic programs, its advertisements, its amusements, its culture, its treatment of nature. . . .
>
> Because the university occupies a strategic place in the institutions which exist to justify irrationality, the political

system will be forced to politicize it, wherever it is located and no matter what its prestige. The university is the place where those who could be most expected to perceive irrationality congregate; this means that the American university is inherently engaged in consciousness-manipulation. It does this through its course work, in social science courses which often teach that all is well, in art courses which tend to avoid the very real art of the inarticulate until it becomes historically interesting, in literature courses which define the work of members of historical elites as the only "real" literature. It does this through its governance, socializing the young adult who passes through it into passivity, the acceptance of authoritarian structures. It does this through its rules of success, reinforcing careerism and cynicism, discouraging theoretical thinking so often, encouraging competitiveness and individualism so frequently. In short, without being part of a conscious conspiracy to win acceptance for present political arrangements, the American university has inevitably become politicized. Its function is to rationalize, and this it does well.

Or did well. The spring events have started a process which may unwind the cycle. For once, the reality of American political life broke through all the attempts to cover it. Those students and faculty who perceived this and did something about their perception were not politicizing the university, as many seem to feel, but giving it its first real chance to depoliticize itself.[17]

If Wolfe's view articulated a radical critique of the university echoed by many in today's protest movements, the AAUP also offered space to more cautious responses. Samuel Krislov, a political scientist at the University of Minnesota, wrote that

radical ideas . . . deserve our fair-minded consideration and discussion, both as systems of ideas and as individual proposals. But radical proposals are also programmatic. At least some of these proposals involve moving to institutional affirmations of truth and the use of collective action as leverage—student power to help mobilize faculty power to commit universities to influence society. . . .

Should we take it upon ourselves collectively and officially to push our society to accept policies, and to use institutional leverage even to try to force policy change—a current foolish but flattering misperception of our influence—we will have thereby lost our individual claim to academic freedom.[18]

Perhaps more stridently, political scientists Guenter Lewy and Stanley Rothman also pushed back against the potential problems for the faculty's academic freedom posed by demands for student power. "A democratic political system aims at the well-being of its people, and no citizen, no matter how wealthy or clever, has a monopoly of knowledge in the ways of attaining this goal," they wrote.

On the other hand, certain institutions within a democratic society do have clearly defined purposes, and these, to be attained, require skill, knowledge, and experience. . . . The university's special mission requires the authority of the teacher, and the communication of knowledge is impossible without hierarchy and discipline. The different roles which professors and students play in the university are built into the essence of the institution. . . . Though universities are no more likely than other human institutions to achieve perfection, there is no reason why . . . principles of academic freedom should now be compromised or surrendered to students whose competence to decide questions of educational policy or academic personnel is no greater than that of earlier challengers of academic freedom.[19]

By the mid-1970s, student unrest had waned, but a series of incidents in which speakers were disrupted by protests prompted Yale University's president to empower a faculty committee, chaired by historian C. Vann Woodward, to examine free speech issues. That committee's 1974 report took a position clearly critical of student protest. It began auspiciously, declaring that a university's "primary function . . . is to discover and disseminate knowledge by means of research and teaching," for which "the right to think the unthinkable, discuss the unmentionable, and challenge the unchallengeable" is essential. But the report quickly jumped from that unassailable contention to claim that "the paramount obligation of the university is to protect the right to free expression." This muddles the difference between academic freedom, based on the disciplinary and professional expertise of the faculty, and freedom of speech, a civil and political liberty enjoyed by all in the public arena, including college and university students. It collapses the distinction drawn by Chemerinsky and Gilman between a "professional zone" and a "free speech zone." As Robert Post pointed out, the Woodward report's commitment to research and teaching and its "overriding" commitment to free speech "cannot be reconciled." Moreover, a law student member of the committee dissented from its report, pointing out several "interferences with the free market of ideas at Yale," for which the university administration and not student protesters was responsible.[20]

The 1967 *Joint Statement on Rights and Freedoms of Students*

In 1967, the AAUP joined with other higher education and student groups to issue the *Joint Statement on Rights and Freedoms of Students*, the proclaimed aim of which was "to enumerate the essential provisions for student freedom to learn." The *Statement*, the most thorough presentation of an American version of *Lernfreiheit*, not only protected the free expression rights of students generally but also spoke specifically to student academic freedom in the classroom. It called on the professor to "encourage free discussion, inquiry and expression, [and to evaluate students] solely on an academic basis, not on opinions or conduct in matters unrelated to academic standards." Students should also "have protection through orderly procedures against prejudiced or capricious academic evaluation." Moreover, "information about student views, beliefs, and political associations which professors acquire in the course of their work as instructors, advisers, and counselors should be considered confidential."

The *Statement* addressed students' free speech rights outside the classroom, noting that students "bring to the campus a variety of interests previously acquired and develop many new interests as members of the academic community." They should, therefore, "be free to organize and join associations to promote their common interests." The *Statement* added that "students and student organizations should be free to examine and discuss all questions of interest to them, and to express opinions publicly and privately. They should always be free to support causes by orderly means which do not disrupt the regular and essential operation of the institution."[21]

The *Statement* recognized the right of students to participate in institutional governance: "As constituents of the academic community, students should be free, individually and collectively, to express their views on issues of institutional policy and on matters of general interest to the student body. The student body should have clearly defined means to participate in the formulation and application of institutional policy affecting academic and student affairs." The extent and precise nature of such participation was left unclear, however. Nonetheless, in 1970 an AAUP committee issued the *Draft Statement on Student Participation in College and University Governance*, which proposed that "students should be consulted in decisions regarding the development of already-existing programs and the establishment of new programs." It added that "student opinion should also be consulted, where feasible, in the selection of presidents, chief academic and nonacademic administrative officers, including the dean of students, and faculty."[22]

Paralleling the faculty's academic freedom of extramural expression, the 1967 *Statement* proclaimed that "students are both citizens and members of the academic community" and as citizens "should enjoy the same freedom of speech, peaceful assembly and right of petition that other citizens enjoy." The statement added this essential caution: "Faculty members and administrative officials should insure that institutional powers are not employed to inhibit such intellectual and personal development of students as is often promoted by their exercise of the rights of citizenship both on and off campus."

Student Media

The 1967 *Statement* declared that "student publications and the student press are valuable aids in establishing and maintaining an atmosphere of free and responsible discussion and of intellectual exploration on the campus." Student publications should be "free of censorship and advance approval of copy" and student editors and managers "free to develop their own editorial policies and news coverage," "protected from arbitrary suspension and removal because of student, faculty, administration, or public disapproval of editorial policy or content."

In 2016, the AAUP, the College Media Association, the Student Press Law Center, and the National Coalition Against Censorship issued a report, *Threats to the Independence of Student Media*, which found that "many college and university authorities have exhibited an intimidating level of hostility toward student media, inhibiting the free exchange of ideas on campus." The report called attention not only to a growing number of instances in which student publications were improperly censored but also to cases where faculty media advisers were subject to discipline and even dismissal. "Conducting 'prior review' violates the basic tenets of the college or university media adviser's personal and professional code," the report stated. "Media advisers are, above all else, educators who seek to train young journalists in the practice of ethical, thorough journalism. Typically, they are not producers of college or university journalism and should not be expected—or allowed—to interfere in the editorial process."

Nor should they be subject to discipline for declining to so interfere.

"Student journalists and their faculty advisers work in a gray zone of legal uncertainty," the report continued. The Supreme Court has never addressed whether college and university student journalists should be treated like professionals or whether they have only the minimal rights afforded to high school journalists under the court's 1988 ruling in *Hazelwood School District v. Kuhlmeier*. In that case, the court held that public school student newspapers that are part of a curriculum and have not been specifically established as forums for student expression are subject to a lower level of First Amendment protection than independent student expression or newspapers established as forums for student expression. In a 5-3 decision, the court declared that school administrators could exercise prior restraint of school-sponsored expression, such as curriculum-based student newspapers and assembly speeches, if the censorship is "reasonably related to legitimate pedagogical concerns." Federal appeals courts have been divided on whether *Hazelwood* applies to college newspapers, a question the Supreme Court did not address. "Although a handful of states have clarified and fortified the rights of college and university journalists by way of state statute, few extend that enhanced protection to faculty advisers," the report noted.[23]

Students as Teachers and Researchers

For most graduate students and a small number of undergraduates, research and teaching play critical roles in their educations. The question thus arises as to whether in their capacities as instructors, teaching assistants, or researchers such students may claim the academic freedom rights accorded to faculty in those spheres. In 2000, the AAUP approved the *Statement on Graduate Students*, which recognized that graduate assistants "carry out many of the functions of faculty members and receive compensation for these duties." It declared, "Graduate students have the right to academic freedom. . . . they should be able to express their opinions freely about matters of institutional policy, and they should have the same freedom of action in the public political domain as faculty members should have. Graduate students' freedom of inquiry is necessarily qualified by their still being learners in the profession; nonetheless, their faculty mentors should afford them latitude and respect as they decide how they will engage in teaching and research." The *Statement* added that "graduate students are entitled to the protection of their intellectual-property rights, including recognition of their participation in supervised research and their research with faculty."

The *Statement* does not, however, directly address the rights of graduate students when they are instructors of record and not merely assistants in a course. In such cases these students become contingent employees, with full rights to academic freedom no different from those of other faculty members. Indeed, it is often the case that a graduate student at one institution may serve simultaneously as a part-time non-tenure-track instructor at another. Hence, the AAUP treats graduate student instructors of record as members of the faculty, and it has also endorsed the right of graduate student employees to unionize and engage in collective bargaining.

In 2002, the English Department at Berkeley listed a section of a course in basic reading and writing skills entitled "The Politics and Poetics of Palestinian Resistance," to be taught by a graduate student. The course description clearly evidenced the instructor's partisan viewpoint and closed with the warning that "conservative thinkers are encouraged to seek other sections." Controversy erupted, and the department worked with the student instructor to modify the description, which had clearly stepped beyond the bounds of academic freedom. A new description, which still made clear the instructor's viewpoint, was approved by the Academic Senate. Concerns remained, however, that tension between the instructor's academic freedom right to approach his subject from a perspective he espoused and the right of students to register their disagreement with that perspective might not be properly resolved. As a consequence, the department and instructor agreed that a tenured member of the faculty would observe the class to ensure fairness.[24]

In 2018, the AAUP investigated the case of a sixth-year doctoral student with a part-time appointment as lecturer at the University of Nebraska-Lincoln. The graduate student instructor had participated in a spontaneous demonstration at a recruiting table for the conservative organization Turning Point, USA, sponsor of the Professor Watchlist, staffed at the time by an undergraduate. Within hours, a video taken by the undergraduate had gone viral, and the graduate student instructor began receiving online threats, while the administration received calls for her dismissal. Treating the graduate student instructor as "a faculty member," whose behavior was "unprofessional" and "not in keeping with the standards of conduct," the administration removed her, with pay, from her teaching responsibilities, allegedly for "security reasons." The suspension continued for the remainder of the academic year, constituting in the AAUP's eyes a summary dismissal.

The AAUP investigation found that political pressure played a part in the case. "In the days immediately following the release of the video, Republican members of the Nebraska legislature began pressuring the university to remove [the graduate student lecturer] from the classroom and terminate her contract. The evidence suggests that criticism from conservative state politicians helped keep the incident in the public eye." With respect to academic freedom, the investigation concluded "that the administration dismissed [the instructor] for reasons associated with the political content of her speech . . . given the varying statements made by the administration—at the campus and system level—about the nature of her misconduct and evidence concerning the political pressure exerted on the university." In this case both the university and the AAUP treated the graduate student as an instructor on a term contract. It is unclear how the case might have unfolded had the university responded to the incident by instead applying student disciplinary policies as if this were simply a dispute between two students.[25]

In Loco Parentis Redivivus?

In 2020, a massive movement to remove public monuments to tarnished figures from the national past, especially leaders of the Confederacy and other promoters of racial slavery, swept the nation. Despite a handful of excesses, that movement rightfully won broad popular support. Its origins, as with so many other modern social movements, may be traced to college and university campuses, for instance, the prolonged and ultimately successful struggle to remove Silent Sam, an especially odious Confederate commemoration, from the campus of the University of North Carolina.[26] The monuments movement was part of a broader campus engagement with problems of racism, historic and contemporary, once again led by Black and other students of color. It can be dated at least from the 2015 upheaval at the University of Missouri, which toppled system and campus leaders and cost a probationary faculty member her job—in violation of her academic freedom—in the political backlash that followed.[27]

With the revival of student activism, many of the themes of the 1960s and 1970s responses were revived as well. While most faculty members have been sympathetic to student activism, some bemoan the spread of an alleged "political correctness" or "cancel culture" and have sometimes marshaled claims of free speech against dissenting expression that is merely disorderly. Taking the place of Yale's Woodward Report has been the University of Chicago's 2015 report from a committee on free expression, commonly known as the Chicago Principles, since endorsed by dozens of college and university administrations nationwide. That report reviewed university policies on free expression, but made no mention of academic freedom in the classroom or in research. It declared that "the University's fundamental commitment is to the principle that debate or deliberation may not be suppressed because the ideas put forth are thought by some or even by most members of the University community to be offensive, unwise, immoral, or wrong-headed." But the report appeared to give equal emphasis to another principle—that "members of the University community must also act in conformity with the principle of free expression"—leading many to believe that its chief import was to validate suppression of potentially disruptive protest, especially demonstrations against controversial outside speakers.

In several states legislation was introduced that allegedly aimed to "restore and protect freedom of thought and expression on campus," but would mandate harsh disciplinary policies for students "who interfere with the free expression of others." These laws were critiqued extensively in reports by PEN America and the AAUP. In 2017, the AAUP declared its strong support for "freedom of expression on campus and the rights of faculty and students to invite speakers of their choosing." Gesturing to the principles of the 1966 *Statement on Governance* and to the courts' doctrine of institutional academic freedom, the AAUP further declared its opposition to "any legislation that interferes with the institutional autonomy of colleges and universities by undermining the role of faculty, administration, and governing board in institutional decision-making and the role of students in the formulation and application of institutional policies affecting student affairs."[28]

Such legislative proposals to a great extent recapitulate the 1970 Nixon commission's effort to shift attention from the serious critique of societal and educational policies and practices offered by the protests to the behavior and occasional excesses of the protesters. But if the 1970 response led to abandonment of *in loco parentis*, the recent reaction tends to reinforce that principle, consistent with already developing trends in response to other concerns. Since the 1980s, fears about legal liability and an increasingly consumerist approach to both the marketing and the structure of higher education have led higher education administrations to reembrace a modified version of *in loco parentis.*[29]

In the wake of a perceived increase in campus crime, expanded awareness of problems associated with student sexual violence and harassment, often linked to alcohol abuse, and widespread reports of fraternity hazing tragedies and misbehavior by student athletes, school administrations—as well as courts and governments—"have increasingly recognized a college's duty to provide a safe learning environment both on and off campus."[30] This has led to a growing tendency to police student conduct—but also student expression—in the name of "safety," especially as student protests reemerged, and to the creation of ever-expanding bureaucracies dedicated to enforcing an expansive ideal of security with serious ramifications for student academic freedom. In one almost Orwellian move, a committee at the University of Chicago proposed protecting free speech by creating "free speech deans-on-call . . . to deal with disruptive conduct." As law professor Jeannie Suk Gersen commented, such "bureaucratic responses . . . mirror what many universities have done in recent years to address bias and discrimination."[31]

The institution of campus speech codes, ostensibly aimed at curbing alleged hate speech directed at minorities, can be seen as one example. While these could receive powerful justification as an important mechanism for ensuring "an atmosphere respectful of and welcoming to all persons," the AAUP concluded in 1992 that "rules that ban or punish speech based upon its content cannot be justified. An institution of higher learning fails to fulfill its mission if it asserts the power to proscribe ideas— and racial or ethnic slurs, sexist epithets, or homophobic insults almost always express ideas, however repugnant. Indeed, by proscribing any ideas, a university sets an example that profoundly disserves its academic mission."[32]

Courts have repeatedly struck down campus speech codes as overly broad. At the same time, however, they have "continued to widen the scope of colleges' duty of care over their students."[33] Greg Lukianoff, executive director of the Foundation for Individual Rights in Education, has demonstrated how colleges and universities have created an "expanding bureaucracy" with "responsibility for writing and enforcing speech codes, creating speech zones, and policing students' lives in ways that students from the 1960s would never have accepted." As colleges and universities are run more like businesses in search of revenue from student "customers," the pressure to please those customers intensifies. But students are not customers. The notion that they are and must be pleased arises inevitably from the idea that higher education is not about the public good, but about individual private improvement. Lukianoff concludes that "administrators have been successful in convincing students that the primary goal of the university is to make students feel comfortable. Unfortunately, comfortable minds are often not thinking ones." One political scientist agrees, noting that "the hunt to root out microaggressions and supposedly traumatizing speech originate from the bloated administrative wing of campus."[34] When this is combined with the judiciary's emphasis on protecting the academic freedom of institutions over that of faculty members and students, the free speech gains of the 1960s and 1970s stand in danger of further erosion.

Student protesters may at times appear intemperate, intolerant, or simply immature. Protests do at times interfere with the freedoms of others, including the academic freedom of individual faculty members. But we should heed the words of conservative scholar Jonathan Marks: "Whatever closed-mindedness students exhibit isn't obviously worse than that of their elders. Whatever suspicion students have of the glories of speech and debate is partly justified by the stupidity and insincerity of what passes for public discussion." Moreover, whatever excesses they may now and then commit, whatever violations of the free expression of others they may occasionally advocate or attempt to impose, student activists more often than not do more to advance not only the causes they espouse but also the cause of free expression itself than do those who run their colleges and universities and many of the faculty who teach in them. As the faculty editors of a recent symposium on student protest noted, students "come to our campuses to 'get an education'; yet many of them, without the cover of tenure or prestige, give us an education on courage."[35]

Student activism is about politics, citizenship, critical engagement with the institution of the university, and the exercise of freedom of speech in the tradition of the FSM. But it is also itself a kind of learning activity and, in the final analysis, if "student academic freedom" means anything, it is about the freedom to learn, about *Lernfreiheit*.

Chapter 8

Knowledge

- -

❝I thought it was a hoax." Those were among the final words spoken by a 30-year-old man to medical personnel before his death. He had reported attending a "COVID-19 party," at which attendees allegedly mingled with someone who tested positive for the virus to determine for themselves if the threat was real.[1] This was but one tragic incident among many as Americans paid a steep price for the hostility to science, expertise, and intellectual engagement that has long plagued our country, from the tavern to the White House. Those who refused to listen to and even politically attacked expert epidemiologists in 2020 were preceded by politicians and business leaders—and, unfortunately, some academics—who, for decades, denied the reality of human-caused climate change and sought to discredit climate scientists, voiced unfounded skepticism about the effects of preventive vaccinations, or denied the cancer-causing consequences of tobacco smoke while secretly receiving "research" grants from cigarette manufacturers.

Insofar as threats to academic freedom have a political coloration, they have been and likely will continue to be bipartisan. The assault on science and expert knowledge is likewise deeply rooted in traditions of anti-intellectualism, entwined with the country's toxic heritage of racism and acquisitive individualism, which span the political spectrum. Nonetheless, in recent years the political assault on science has for the most part been driven by powerful interests—energy firms, whose profits are threatened by responses to climate change, some anti-abortion activists, and "creationist" evangelical ideologues—concentrated in the Republican Party. In a 2017 report, *National Security, the Assault on Science, and Academic Freedom*, the AAUP documented a broad array of examples of the politicization of science in both the George W. Bush and Trump administrations.[2] These include manipulation of scientific advisory committees, distortion and suppression of scientific information, restrictions on international scientific exchange, and interference with scientific research and analysis. In a 2019 report, the Union of Concerned Scientists concluded prophetically that the Trump administration had demonstrated "a pervasive pattern of sidelining science in critical decisionmaking, compromising our nation's ability to meet current and future public health and environmental challenges."[3]

The AAUP report also noted how "some private individuals have at times made threats and engaged in various forms of online and other harassment against scientists and faculty members whose research, teaching, or public commentary run against their own cherished beliefs, notably in the field of climate science." The report also decried how "a more general outlook that associates scientific work with subversion, threatens academic freedom. Indeed, that outlook—profoundly anti-intellectual, invoking anti-elitism as its mantra—makes the attacks on individuals possible." As Ernst Benjamin points out, "scientific disputes inherent in exploring and testing new scientific understandings have long been used as a cover for politically motivated, unscientific efforts to discredit otherwise sound science."[4]

The Assault on Expertise and Learning

Attacks on science must be understood as part of a broader assault on expertise and intellect and on the colleges and universities in which they can most freely function. As Robert Post worries, "the infinite gush of information now cheaply and easily available on the internet has made every person an authority on every subject. The upshot is that for many, truth is no longer the product of patient inquiry and disciplinary craft. It is instead merely an opinion produced in the echo chambers of like-minded partisans." Moreover, such opinions often exhibit "no respect for claims to knowledge that are validated by practices of craft and method." They have "no respect for the independent status of facts."[5]

In January 2020, the AAUP released a major statement, *In Defense of Knowledge and Higher Education*, which would quickly be endorsed by a variety of higher education groups, including the American Federation of Teachers, the American Historical Association, the Association of American Colleges and Universities, the American Society of Journalists and Authors, the Association of University Presses, PEN America, and the Phi Beta Kappa Society. The statement situated the assault on scientific knowledge within "an ongoing movement to attack the disciplines and institutions that produce and transmit the knowledge that sustains American democracy."[6]

"No state can organize effective government policy except on the basis of informed, dispassionate investigation," the statement explained. It asked, "How can we develop a credible foreign policy, ensure effective diplomacy, and prepare our military when area studies and foreign language programs are curtailed, eliminated, or made subject to political intrusion?" It argued that "a narrowing focus on vocational training, combined with attacks on the liberal arts and general education, closes off access to the varieties of knowledge and innovative thinking needed to participate meaningfully in our democracy."

"Expert knowledge is not produced in a 'marketplace of ideas' in which all opinions are equally valid," the statement continued. "The dialogue that produces expert knowledge occurs among those who are qualified by virtue of their training, education, and disciplinary practice." In this light, the statement decried "an explicit political campaign attacking universities as enemies of freedom of speech. Since all are equally entitled to freedom of speech, scholarly standards and criteria are attacked as mere intimidation and unjustifiable censorship." As this book argues, freedom of speech and academic freedom must not be confused. The former is a right, a precious right, available to all. But "expert knowledge is . . . not produced by simple freedom of speech. A major symptom of our contemporary crisis is that some nevertheless seek to subordinate expert knowledge to public opinion." Expert knowledge is protected not by freedom of speech but by academic freedom.

In 1902, John Dewey proclaimed that "it is practically impossible for any serious question regarding academic freedom to arise in the sphere of mathematics, astronomy, physics, or chemistry. . . . The biological sciences are clearly in a transitional state. The conception of evolution is a test case." Yet, even here, Dewey maintained that "little sympathy could be secured for an attack upon a university for encouraging the use of this theory." More than a century later his claims sound unduly confident. Dewey's purpose, however, was to distinguish these sciences from

> another group of sciences, which from the standpoint of definitive method and a clearly accepted body of verified fact are more remote from a scientific status. I refer especially to the social and psychological disciplines. . . . To the public at large the facts and relations with which these topics deal are still almost wholly in the region of opinion, prejudice, and accepted tradition. . . . The general public may be willing enough to admit in the abstract the existence of a science of political economy, sociology, or psychology,

but when these dare to emerge from a remote and technical sphere, and pass authoritative judgment upon affairs of daily life . . . they meet with little but skepticism or hostility or, what is worse, sensational exploitation.[7]

While it may no longer be fashionable to refer to these disciplines as sciences, Dewey used the term in the sense of the German *Wissenschaft*, and his point remains valid. If the physical and biological sciences that he believed were largely immune from assault are today subject to intense disbelief and denigration, social science disciplines are in an even more vulnerable position. Because "political economy, sociology, historical interpretation, psychology . . . deal with problems of life, not problems of technical theory," Dewey wrote, "the right and duty of academic freedom are even greater here than elsewhere."

The humanities, too, are under assault as elitist, if not simply irrelevant. While most of the public will at least begrudgingly defer to experts in medicine, one scholar has noted, "it's resistant to the very possibility that expertise exists in fields like literature ('you just read books and give your opinion') or philosophy ('navel-gazing')."[8] Yet these disciplines, which depend on critical inquiry and hermeneutic interpretation rather than experimentation and analysis of data, also develop and transmit expert knowledge. To be sure, they regularly produce conflicting views, each of which may claim validity. Such is often also the case, however, in the social and even the physical sciences, as debates over how best to deal with the COVID-19 pandemic revealed. If humanists may be reluctant to call themselves experts, their work still reflects expertise. That expertise is founded on knowledge of and familiarity with the material studied. Much as a radiologist analyzing an x-ray knows what to look for and what may be revealed, so too a close student of, say, eighteenth-century poetry will quickly recognize and comprehend language that might appear impenetrable to a layperson. Two scholars may advance diametrically opposed interpretations of a work of literature or art, or of the import and value of an artistic or literary tradition, but each brings to their interpretation years of training and study that mark their views as more than mere opinion. Expertise, therefore, should not be construed as the plain accumulation of factual knowledge or "the simple transmission and application of a method."[9]

"Colleges and universities need to take responsibility for protecting and expanding knowledge that cannot be translated into commercial terms," Michael Meranze writes in the wake of the pandemic. "Current national and global struggles over policing and statues, over the inheritances of colonialism or the values of knowledge itself, point to the central role of the humanities and the social sciences in understandings of the everyday world. Still, the need to acknowledge the public functions of scientific knowledge has never been clearer than it is today."[10]

In all disciplines, scholars regularly engage in debate, recognizing that while facts may be indisputable, meaning and understanding are of necessity always uncertain and developing, emerging out of ongoing and never-ending conversations in disciplinary communities. These will never be entirely inextricable from the political environment in which they take place. Academic freedom, however, strives as much as possible to insulate such conversations from being unduly politicized, especially through external interference and pressure. As Post argues, "the effort to protect the integrity of disciplinary knowledge grows more important now as our political life grows more tribal." In such a context, academic freedom stands as a guardian of "the possibility of constructive political dialogue" if not an assurance of the naive belief that scholarship must or even can ever be free of politics.[11]

Defunding Higher Education

The contemporary assault on expert knowledge, intellect, and higher learning is incomprehensible outside the context of profound changes in the economy of higher education, which some have deemed "neoliberalism" but which can also be described, in Joy Connolly's words, as "the corruption of institutions by money."[12] Or, perhaps more accurately, by the search for money. *In Defense of Knowledge* noted that in the aftermath of World War II, the United States invested heavily in higher education as a public good, albeit not always equitably. Beginning in the 1970s, however, "the commitment to producing knowledge as a public good began to wane." Declines in federal and state support began just as the civil rights and women's movements pried open higher education to previously underserved groups. "Public higher education has undergone a financial and conceptual shift," journalist Scott Carlson wrote. "Once an investment covered mostly by the state to produce a workforce and an informed citizenry, today it is more commonly shouldered by individuals and families and described as a private benefit, a means to a credential and a job." He adds, "As the student population has diversified, the language that many people use to define the value of a college degree has shifted, from a public good to an individual one. Is that merely a coincidence?"[13]

According to one study, from 2003 to 2013 state support for public research universities declined by 28 percent on a perstudent basis. As late as 2018, nearly a third of the fifty states had decreased higher education funding. In the country's largest fouryear public system, the California State University, between 1985 and 2015 state funding fell by 2.9 percent in constant dollars, even as the system added more than 150,000 full-time equivalent students. Since 1982, one report found, 80 percent of new white enrollments went to the 468 most selective colleges, but 72 percent of new Latinx and 68 percent of new Black enrollment went to two-year and four-year open-access institutions, which have the fewest resources. As Christopher Newfield concludes, "The purpose of privatization is to move resources toward those willing to pay for them, which in practice means giving more to those with more, and giving less to those with less."[14]

One consequence of these trends has been the growing emphasis on training for careers over educating for citizenship and life as central to higher education's mission. Degrees are promoted more as credentials for employment than markers of educational attainment. As the pursuit of learning takes a back seat to the pursuit of work, the faculty's central role in setting the direction of and governing the university erodes. For those who run the institution, access to funding increasingly becomes the mission rather than a means to fulfilling the mission. The quest for increased tuition dollars, supported by skyrocketing student debt, and the "entrepreneurial" search for outside research funding described in chapter 2, merge to yield a common erosion of free inquiry and democratic education. As a consequence, *In Defense of Knowledge* declared, "The faith that American higher education produces expert knowledge that benefits the entire society has diminished. Indeed, the unequal and unfair distribution of educational opportunity may well have played a significant role in making expertise appear more like a privilege of the wealthy and an expression of their interests than a disinterested contribution to the public good."

But it would be wrong to blame the public. As Newfield has argued, "Privatization came from senior politicians and their business allies . . . there was no voter shift away from public goods." Instead, "there was an abandonment of the political fight for them by academic managers."[15] A 2019 survey of 1,400 likely voters found that strong majorities believed that bachelor's and associate's degrees are "worth the investment and usually" pay off (70 and 69 percent, respectively) and that most higher education institutions "provide a high-quality education to their students" (72 percent). When asked how best to define higher education's purpose, 58 percent said it should both "set students up for success in their careers" and "broaden the perspectives of students and make them better and more informed citizens," while 24 percent cited only the former purpose and 11 percent only the latter.[16] Another survey of more than five thousand respondents conducted on behalf of the American Academy of Arts and Sciences found that 56 percent of Americans agree strongly that "the humanities should be an important part of every American's education," while 38 percent "somewhat agreed" with that statement. The survey also reported that 78 percent of Americans wish they had taken more courses in a humanities-related subject and nearly half wish they'd taken more classes in languages other than English.[17]

"Cautious administrators who fear offending students and their tuition-paying parents and business-minded boards," Connolly notes, are increasingly ill-equipped and poorly situated to defend either academic freedom or the pursuit of knowledge itself. Requiring "efficient business operations is one thing," she adds. "To conceive of . . . the university itself as a business in a fundamental sense . . . is different."[18] If we accept the idea that education is only about career—or, even worse, about getting an entry-level job—we lose sight of what education is truly about, and we engage in a fundamentally anti-intellectual activity that should be alien to higher education.

Anti-intellectualism

The assault on knowledge and its consequent negative impact on academic freedom cannot be disentangled from longstanding American suspicions of the intellectual life. The standard treatment of this trend has been Richard Hofstadter's *Anti-Intellectualism in American Life* (1964), a flawed but brilliant work, many of whose insights remain compelling. "Much of what American intellectuals these days seem to find shocking would not surprise Hofstadter in the slightest," Nicholas Lemann wrote in 2014. "The Tea Party movement, or people who refuse to vaccinate their children against diseases, or the idea of paying schoolteachers on the basis of numerical measures of how well they confer skills to their students" are all developments for which Hofstadter found historical precedent. One of his many insights was that as the economic, political, and cultural roles of "trained intelligence" have increased over time, "jocular and usually benign ridicule of intellect and formal training has turned into a malign resentment of the intellectual in his capacity as expert."

While expert advice has always been essential to democratic governance, the populist conviction of the anti-intellectual—that experts and bureaucrats have surreptitiously seized power from the people, which Hofstadter traced to the Progressive Era and especially the New Deal—is at best a half-truth. New Deal reforms "pleased the intellectuals," but they were enacted "not because the experts favored them but because some large constituency wanted them." Still, it was possible then, as it is now, to perceive intellectuals—and the colleges and universities that house them—as a privileged elite governing not in the interest of the great majority but on their own behalf. In that light, claims to academic freedom are taken as claims of immunity to popular accountability.[19]

It would be difficult to deny that populist trends in culture and religion have in the past and still now play a role in anti-intellectual assaults on expertise, higher education, and academic freedom, but these have most often been empowered by those with formidable economic and political clout. Indeed, in Hofstadter's account, business was portrayed as the dominant element in American culture and businessmen as a major source of anti-intellectualism. Today, alleged grassroots movements are often really "astroturf" movements, funded and created by potent moneyed and politically connected interests. Mass online harassment of controversial professors may sometimes originate spontaneously, but it is fueled overwhelmingly by well-funded organizations financed by well-heeled donors. Opposition to climate change research is almost entirely the creation of fossil fuel producers. "It is difficult to get a man to understand something when his salary depends upon his not understanding it," the socialist Upton Sinclair famously declared. It is even more difficult, however, if his profit margin and capital gains depend on it.

Hofstadter almost totally missed the central role played by race and racism in American history and in the development of an anti-intellectual culture and of resistance to it. He "hardly mentioned the significant intellectual movements in support of rights for African-Americans and women, and he mostly ignored the rebirth of these movements at the time he was writing."[20] In this, it might be said, Hofstadter demonstrated the anti-intellectualism of intellectuals who fail to acknowledge the intellectual life of non-elites. This points to an important lesson. Insofar as the developments chronicled above have led to an overly practical and anti-intellectual vision of education, the answer is not to retreat into an ivory tower, where ideas are enshrined as unchanging truths, but to engage the world by applying intellect while respecting and even learning from the lives, understandings, and experiences of others, not least of all students.

Postmodernism

It has become something of a cliché to argue that the academy itself must bear much of the blame for the assault on knowledge, owing not only to its inequities and tendencies toward elitism but also to corrosive trends in scholarship. There may be some truth to this, but the idea that a persistent epistemological and moral relativism—represented by the much misunderstood and now largely pejorative sobriquet of postmodernism—has been a major culprit is at best greatly exaggerated. In 1996, physicist Alan Sokal submitted an article to *Social Text*, an academic journal of cultural studies. The article proposed that quantum gravity is a social and linguistic construct. At that time the journal did not practice academic peer review and did not submit the article for outside expert reading by a physicist. Soon after publication, Sokal revealed that the article was a hoax, a mishmash of scientific terms and intellectual gibberish designed to expose the claims of the postmodernists. The hoax caused considerable controversy, and for many the article's acceptance was a damning condemnation not only of postmodern relativist thinking but also of scholarly rigor in the humanities more generally—although given the success of hoaxes in the physical sciences recounted briefly in chapter 2, it was actually not all that impressive. A subsequent 2018 "Sokal squared" hoax, in which several bogus articles in gender and critical race studies were accepted—but also rejected—by journals, had less impact, however.[21]

The Sokal hoax shed light on relativistic or "antinomian" intellectual trends, which some charge undermine scholarship's truth claims.[22] "Postmodern theory," Aaron Hanlon tells us, "may be the most loathed concept ever to have emerged from academia" because "it supposedly told us that facts were debatable, that individual perspectives mattered most, that shared meaning was an illusion and that universal truth was a myth." According to Andrew Perrin, postmodernism was charged with having "cultivated a decadent skepticism that served to detach perspective, interpretation, and reception from concrete reality," in the process reducing "scientific and political facts to competing political positions."[23]

These descriptions, however, are themselves little more than political postures, examples of what one scholar called "cartoonish academic politics."[24] Insofar as some relatively coherent trend by that name ever existed, postmodernism's heyday came in the 1980s and 1990s, but even then its relativism was descriptive, not prescriptive. Moreover, the postmodernist label has been attached to people who "share neither intellectual outlook nor research questions, nor disciplinary background, nor the kinds of places they publish," as one historian of science observed. "I'm not saying there are not interconnections among these fields, but lumping them together and just calling them postmodernists, relativists, and their fellow travelers is really loose. It gets close to being a kind of academic McCarthyism, and it really is not something that is intellectually or ethically justifiable."[25]

Insofar as postmodernism was a distinctive intellectual trend, its project was to analyze an intellectual and cultural landscape in which "claims, beliefs, and symbols are tied up with the structures of power and representation that give rise to them." That, however, was never an assertion that all claims and beliefs are equally valid, either epistemologically or morally, and certainly not a celebration of that landscape. "This insight is hardly an assault on truth," writes Perrin. "It's a sober reckoning with the empirical realities of truth creation in our times."

The most unsubstantiated, but still widespread, charge has been that postmodernism, largely a phenomenon of the Left and often conflated with the disciplines of ethnic and gender studies, somehow gave rise to the trope of "fake news" and Trumpian denials of reality, on the Right. If those on the Right who attack expert knowledge employ relativistic arguments, however, they didn't get them from postmodernist scholarship or, for that matter, from any scholarship at all. "I never heard anything remotely postmodern from a member of Congress," commented physicist Steven Weinberg. "I think the forces against taking climate change seriously are overwhelmingly economic. It's like the question of whether tobacco smoke is bad for you or whether sugary sodas are bad for you. All these things are opposed by people who have a financial stake." As scholarship has largely moved on, absorbing the insights of postmodernism's heyday, the label has become for all intents and purposes meaningless, a "zombie idea," which still perversely preoccupies anti-intellectuals who, in Hofstadter's words, have long been "obsessively engaged with this or that outworn or rejected idea."[26]

Those who blame postmodernism and other allegedly relativist intellectual trends for the assault on knowledge and expertise are more often than not facilitating that assault, sometimes even challenging the academic freedom of those they critique. If in the 1950s the argument was that Communists were not entitled to academic freedom because they were beholden to the Party's version of truth, some critics of postmodernism appear to suggest that those they label postmodernists should not be entitled to academic freedom because they allegedly deny the very existence of truth. Looking back after twenty years on his hoax, Sokal acknowledged, "There is in American culture a persistent anti-intellectual current, which looks down on the pointy-headed professors and is happy to pick up on any excuse to have a laugh at them. That was the negative side" of his gambit.[27]

Race, Knowledge, and Academic Freedom

Insofar as public skepticism of higher education's truth-seeking mission can be justified, some fault may lie with the inherently conservative politicization of the university to which Alan Wolfe called attention in 1970. Dewey and his colleagues envisioned the university as a base for political and social reform, but it also inevitably functions to maintain and rationalize the existing order, even as many of those who teach and conduct research within its walls develop critiques of that order. Like all established and corporate bodies, the faculty may unconsciously and despite good intentions function as a closed estate, abusing its professional authority in order to preserve its own endangered privileges. As Newfield has pointed out, the professoriate has failed—across the political spectrum—fully to correct for its own inherent biases and interests. In particular, he calls out "the whiteness of tenured faculty ranks, which has been sustained across the many decades since racial integration became a formal societal goal."

"Whatever racial justice we demand for society we don't seem to demand for ourselves," he bemoans. "If this is the case, then why fight to protect professional judgment from external threat?" If the problem "comes from inside the house," then does academic freedom become "a somewhat undeserved buffer from pressures for positive change?" No, Newfield forcefully responds, "there's no evidence that academic freedom as such is the primary cause of the whiteness of the senior faculty" or of other academic ills. Indeed, the real causes lie with developments that "limit the ability of academic freedom as a set of material practices to enable the pursuit of truth and justice at the same time."[28]

Newfield's linkage of truth and justice recalls how the founding of the AAUP and the initial development of the American version of academic freedom grew out of two distinct but complementary impulses, the search for disciplinary and professional authority, on the one hand, and a broader progressive movement seeking to expand democracy in both state and society, on the other hand. As Matthew C. Moen put it, higher education's educational mission "consists of two contradictory yet complementary streams: the pursuit of truth and the creation of virtuous citizens in the community."[29] If academic freedom safeguards the professional rights of teachers and scholars, themselves members of an elite, its justification depends on those professionals' responsibility to serve what both the 1915 *Declaration* and the 1940 *Statement* identified as "the common good" in a democratic society. But just as our understanding of academic freedom has been developed and enriched over the years, so too has our conception of the common good expanded to encompass ever more extensive and engaged versions of democracy.

For academia to rebuild democracy in the university, it must also advance democracy in society—and vice versa. "The challenge of the 2020s will be making the importance of scholarly knowledge clear to an often skeptical if not hostile range of publics," Meranze proposes. "To move toward a relationship with society that emphasizes the joint pursuit of knowledge rather than the transmission of information, higher education will need a new compact with society that is based on its public mission and its public funding. If nothing else, COVID-19 has shown us the devastating inadequacy of a society based on the notion that private goods and interests can meet fundamental collective challenges."[30]

Conclusion

If, as this book has suggested, academic freedom may now be in as much danger as at any time since the dark days of the 1950s anti-Communist hysteria, these words from the AAUP's 1956 investigation of that hysteria's impact on academic freedom seem prescient:

> We cannot censure the justified public interest in colleges and universities, or be unmindful of the extremely difficult task confronting academic administrations that seek to preserve educational and research opportunities in order to serve the general welfare in spite of the suspicions of a public which, at times, has been confused by complicated issues or led astray by demagogic appeals. The temptation to yield a little in order to preserve a great deal is strong, particularly when faculty members who cry out for protection seem willfully uncooperative. Yet to yield a little is, in such matters, to run the risk of sacrificing all. Those who feel safe today may become the victims of tomorrow, just as many of yesterday's political heretics share in today's orthodoxy.
>
> We cannot accept an educational system that is subject to the irresponsible push and pull of contemporary controversies; and we deem it to be the duty of all elements in the academic community—faculty, trustees, officials and, as far as possible, students—to stand their ground firmly even while they seek, with patient understanding, to enlarge and deepen popular comprehension of the nature of academic institutions and of society's dependence upon unimpaired intellectual freedom.[31]

These sentiments are as relevant today as in the 1950s. The authors of the 1915 *Declaration* and all who have followed in their path sought to safeguard professional inquiry and instruction against attacks both overt and covert, in order to ensure that their benefits would be put at the service of democratic governance. Their goals were always in good measure aspirations, but they are aspirations that must continue to guide us.

Appendix

Principles of Academic Freedom

The following principles, extracted from the preceding chapters, are offered as guides to the application of appropriate professional judgment.

- Academic freedom is the collective freedom of the scholarly community to govern itself, in the interest of serving the common good in a democratic society.
- Academic freedom comprises three elements: freedom of inquiry and research, freedom of teaching, and freedom of expression as citizens.
- Academic freedom belongs to the academic profession as a whole to pursue inquiry and teach freely, limited and guided only by the principles of that profession. It is not a civil right like freedom of speech, nor is it simply an individual employment benefit provided to those in a restricted number of academic appointments. Although it grants considerable scope to the consciences of individual scholars, it is not an individual right of professors to do whatever they wish in their research and teaching or to say whatever they might in public remarks.
- There should be no invidious distinctions between those who teach or conduct research in higher education, regardless of whether they hold full-time or part-time appointments or whether their appointments are tenured, tenure-track, or contingent. All faculty members should have access to the same academic freedom and due-process protections and procedures.

Research

- Scholars are entitled to full freedom in research and in the publication of the results, but researchers must conform to accepted intellectual and disciplinary standards. Nowhere in higher education is freedom of inquiry and research totally unrestrained. Restrictions by law and peer review are both common and necessary.
- Legitimate restraints on research can be established and policed only by the community of trained researchers itself. Faculty regulation of research is accomplished mainly through systems of peer review.
- A university's effort to ensure that all researchers comply with its human-subject regulations does not offend academic freedom, but the specific rules adopted by the government or a university to protect human subjects should be examined because they may abridge academic freedom.
- Classified research and all research that cannot be published is inappropriate on a college or university campus.
- Academic freedom leaves it to faculty members to control what to do—or not to do—with the results of their investigations. It does *not*, however, entitle faculty members to sign away their freedom to disseminate research results.
- Academic freedom does not entitle faculty members to ignore financial conflicts of interest. It does not guarantee faculty members the freedom to accept research funding regardless of the conditions attached.
- Whether applied to patentable inventions or material subject to copyright protection, in all forms of faculty research, the faculty member rather than the institution should determine the subject matter, the intellectual approach and direction, and the conclusions, and should control the intellectual property rights.
- Donor funding agreements should be fully transparent and the faculty's rights to both academic freedom and collective control of research efforts must be upheld.
- Where public records requests seek prepublication communications and other unpublished academic research materials,

compelled disclosure would have a severe chilling effect on intellectual debate among researchers and scientists.
- Artistic expression in the classroom, the studio, and the workshop merits the same assurance of academic freedom that is accorded to other scholarly and teaching activities.

Teaching

- Teachers are entitled to freedom in the classroom in discussing their subject, but they should be careful not to persistently introduce material unrelated to their subject.
- The faculty's freedom in the classroom cannot be properly understood apart from its collective authority over the curriculum. The academic freedom of individual faculty members may be limited by the collective responsibility of the faculty for the institution's curriculum.
- In courses for which faculty members are individually responsible, academic freedom protects an instructor's right to select the materials to be used, to determine the approach to the subject and the pedagogical methods to be employed, to design the assignments, and to assess student academic performance and record grades—all without having their decisions subject to the veto of a department chair, dean, or other administrative officer.
- Teachers must educate, not indoctrinate, students. But instructors can assert viewpoints that remain controversial. Indoctrination occurs whenever an instructor insists that students accept *as truth* propositions that are in fact professionally contestable, without allowing students to challenge their validity or advance alternative understandings.
- Teachers are not obliged to strive for some abstract and impractical ideal of "neutrality" or "balance." To demand that all interpretations must be presented is to demand the impossible.
- Teachers should have the same responsibility for selecting and presenting materials in courses offered online as they have in those offered in traditional classrooms.
- Discussions in the classroom are not intended for the public at large. Classroom expression of college and university teachers,

in person or online, should be considered privileged communications. The unauthorized monitoring or recording of classroom discussions violates academic freedom.

- Limitations of academic freedom because of religious or other aims of the institution should be clearly stated in writing at the time of the appointment.

Extramural Expression

- When they speak and write as citizens, faculty members should be free from institutional censorship or discipline. In such expression they should strive to be accurate, exercise appropriate restraint, show respect for the opinions of others, and make every effort to indicate that they are not speaking for the institution.
- As a general rule, public comments made by faculty members as citizens never represent the institution. Hence, an administration need not, and in most cases should not, publicly criticize a faculty member's controversial views.
- A faculty member's expression of opinion as a citizen cannot constitute grounds for dismissal unless it clearly demonstrates the faculty member's unfitness to serve. Extramural statements rarely bear upon a faculty member's fitness. Moreover, a final decision should take into account the faculty member's entire record as a teacher and scholar.
- College and university administrations must apply to a faculty member's statements on social media the same fitness standard appropriate for older formats. They must also defend faculty members against threats directed against them and resist threats and ultimatums directed at the institution.
- Academic boycotts violate academic freedom, but individual faculty members have the right to advocate and participate in such boycotts.
- Administrators with academic responsibilities should be entitled to the same academic freedom rights as faculty members with regard to their extramural expression. Criteria of fitness for an administrative position, however, may differ from those for a faculty position.

Intramural Expression

- Academic freedom must encompass the right of faculty members to express views on matters having to do with their institution and its policies. It is a faculty member's right not only to disagree with administrative decisions but also to criticize them without fear of retaliation or reprimand.
- Faculty members are neither *subordinate* to, nor do they *report* to, members of the administration. The faculty's role in curricular matters and aspects of student life related to the curriculum is and must be independent of the administration.
- Freedom of intramural expression must also include the freedom to organize faculty members to exert their collective power, including through a union.
- Whether or not collective bargaining is protected by statute, faculty members should have unfettered rights to discuss institutional matters in meetings outside those established by the institution, distribute union and other professional literature, wear buttons, tee shirts and similar paraphernalia, circulate and sign petitions, and join together to protest and change institutional policies and practices.

Tenure

- Tenure is a means to certain ends; specifically: (1) freedom of teaching and research and of extramural activities, and (2) a sufficient degree of economic security to make the profession attractive to men and women of ability.
- Tenure provides that once a probationary period is complete, a full-time faculty member may not be dismissed *without adequate cause* or only on account of bona fide financial exigency or program discontinuance. Tenure is thus essentially a guarantee of due process and presumption of innocence. It is not a guarantee of lifetime employment.
- Tenure need not be granted on the basis of a formal and rigorous review process, although most institutions with tenure systems require such a process. It can be acquired automatically, when a faculty member reaches the end of the requisite probationary period.

- Tenure is not limited to those who may hold a specific academic rank or title. Nor is tenure a reward for merit or a symbol of prestige. It simply denotes a continuing appointment, not professional standing.
- Tenure protects academic freedom by ensuring that scholars may be uninhibited in criticizing and advocating controversial changes in accepted theories, widely held beliefs, existing institutions, as well as the policies, programs, and leadership of their own institutions. The existence of a sufficiently large group of tenured faculty can ensure that dissenters and gadflies will have a community of supporters able to advocate on their behalf.
- A bona fide condition of financial exigency justifying dismissal of tenured faculty is defined as "a severe financial crisis that fundamentally compromises the academic integrity of the institution as a whole and that cannot be alleviated by less drastic means."

Students

- Student academic freedom can be said to encompass the rights of students in the classroom and their broader rights to free expression on and off campus.
- In the classroom, professors should encourage free discussion, inquiry and expression, and evaluate students solely on an academic basis, not on opinions or conduct in matters unrelated to academic standards. Students should have protection through orderly procedures against prejudiced or capricious academic evaluation.
- Students should be free to organize and join associations to promote their common interests. Students and student organizations should be free to examine and discuss all questions of interest to them and to express opinions publicly and privately. They should always be free to support and demonstrate on behalf of causes in which they believe.
- Students should be free, individually and collectively, to express their views on issues of institutional policy and on matters of general interest to the student body.

- As citizens, students should enjoy the same freedom of speech, peaceful assembly, and right of petition that other citizens enjoy.
- Student publications should be free of censorship and advance approval of copy. Student editors and managers should be free to develop their own editorial policies and news coverage and be protected from arbitrary suspension and removal because of student, faculty, administration, or public disapproval of editorial policy or content.
- Graduate students have the right to academic freedom. They should be able to express their opinions freely about matters of institutional policy, and they should have the same freedom in the public political domain as faculty members. When graduate students serve as instructors of record, they should be entitled to the same academic freedom rights in the classroom as other faculty members.

Further Reading

The literature on academic freedom, even if one excludes legal treatises, is vast, but if there is a single essential guide it is the AAUP's *Policy Documents and Reports*, now in its eleventh edition. Known colloquially as the Red Book, it collects most of the major documents cited in this book, plus many others, on issues of academic freedom, tenure, and due process; college and university governance; and other topics.

For a penetrating introduction, see Matthew W. Finkin and Robert C. Post, *For the Common Good: Principles of American Academic Freedom*, based largely on AAUP investigative reports, which offers a valuable argument for academic freedom as "the freedom to pursue the scholarly profession according to the standards of that profession." Stanley Fish's *Versions of Academic Freedom: From Professionalism to Revolution*, while marred by its author's idiosyncratic and cramped view of academic freedom as a "guild privilege," offers an informative survey of approaches.

The Development of Academic Freedom in the United States, by Richard Hofstadter and Walter Metzger, published in 1955, remains the sole historical overview. It was republished in separate volumes, with Metzger's volume *Academic Freedom in the Age of the University* being most relevant to the issues covered in this book. On specific topics, see Hans-Joerg Tiede, *University Reform: The Founding of the American Association of University Professors*; Larry Gerber, *The Rise and Decline of Faculty Governance: Professionalization and the Modern American University*; Ellen Schrecker, *No Ivory Tower: McCarthyism and the Universities*; Joy Ann Williamson-Lott, *Jim Crow Campus: Higher Education and the Struggle for a New Southern Social Order*; and

Metzger's extended essay "The 1940 Statement of Principles on Academic Freedom and Tenure," in *Freedom and Tenure in the Academy*, edited by William Van Alstyne, a reprint of the special issue of *Law and Contemporary Problems*, published on the fiftieth anniversary of the *Statement*, which also includes surveys of tenure and academic freedom law by Van Alstyne, Finkin, and Ralph Brown and Jordan Kurland.

On research and intellectual property issues, see the AAUP's 2014 report, *Recommended Principles to Guide Academy-Industry Relationships*; Jacob Rooksby, *The Branding of the American Mind: How Universities Capture, Manage, and Monetize Intellectual Property and Why It Matters*, and Jennifer Washburn, *University Inc.: The Corporate Corruption of Higher Education*.

The essential work on the rise of contingent employment in the academy is Adrianna Kezar, Tom DePaola, and Daniel T. Scott, *The Gig Academy: Mapping Labor in the Neoliberal University*. See also Kim Tolley, ed., *Professors in the Gig Economy: Unionizing Adjunct Faculty in America*; Herb Childress, *The Adjunct Underclass: How America's Colleges Betrayed Their Faculty, Their Students, and Their Mission*; and John G. Cross and Edie N. Goldenbert, *Off-Track Profs: Nontenured Teachers in Higher Education*. Michael Bérubé and Jennifer Ruth, *The Humanities, Higher Education, and Academic Freedom: Three Necessary Arguments* is a concise and important plea for the revitalization of tenure.

Treatments of First Amendment academic freedom include Marjorie Heins, *Priests of Our Democracy: The Supreme Court, Academic Freedom, and the Anti-Communist Purge*; Robert C. Post, *Democracy, Expertise and Academic Freedom: A First Amendment Jurisprudence for the Modern State*; and Philip Lee, *Academic Freedom at American Universities: Constitutional Rights, Professional Norms, and Contractual Duties*.

On student academic freedom and free speech rights, see Erwin Chemerinsky and Howard Gilman, *Free Speech on Campus*; Sigal Ben-Porath, *Free Speech on Campus*; Keith Whittington, *Speak Freely: Why Universities Must Defend Free Speech*; and Roderick A. Ferguson, *We Demand: The University and Student Protests*. On the Berkeley Free Speech Movement, see Robert Cohen and Reginald E. Zelnik, eds., *The Free Speech Movement: Reflections on Berkeley in the 1960s*. On the new *in loco parentis*, see Greg Lukianoff, *Unlearning Liberty: Campus*

Censorship and the End of American Debate. Although not about free expression, Sara Goldrick-Rab's *Paying the Price: College Costs, Financial Aid, and the Betrayal of the American Dream* offers a more realistic and sobering picture of today's college student than the Ivy League fantasy too often portrayed in the media.

The academic freedom implications of disputes about the academic boycott of Israel are discussed from a liberal Zionist perspective in Kenneth S. Stern, *The Conflict over the Conflict: The Israel-Palestine Campus Debate*. For a different perspective, see the essays in David Landy, Ronit Lentin, and Conor McCarthy, eds., *Enforcing Silence: Academic Freedom, Palestine, and the Criticism of Israel*. The 2013 volume of the AAUP's online *Journal of Academic Freedom* includes several articles and responses on the boycott movement reflecting views both opposing and supporting the AAUP's position.

On free speech generally, with some reference to academic freedom, see Timothy Garton Ash, *Free Speech: Ten Principles for a Wired World*; Suzanne Nossel, *Dare to Speak: Defending Free Speech for All*; and Lee C. Bollinger and Geoffrey R. Stone, eds., *The Free Speech Century*.

Additional recent surveys of note include Akeel Bilgrami and Jonathan Cole, eds., *Who's Afraid of Academic Freedom?*; James L. Turk, ed., *Academic Freedom in Conflict: The Struggle over Free Speech Rights in the University*; Beshara Doumani, ed., *Academic Freedom after September 11*; Robert M. O'Neil, *Academic Freedom in a Wired World*; Joan Wallach Scott, *Knowledge, Power, and Academic Freedom*; and Henry Reichman, *The Future of Academic Freedom*.

Although it does not directly discuss academic freedom, Christopher Newfield's *The Great Mistake: How We Wrecked Public Universities and How We Can Fix Them* provides essential contemporary context.

Acknowledgments

For the past decade I have had the privilege of serving in the national leadership of the AAUP and as chair of its Committee A. My largest debt, therefore, is to the devoted AAUP staff and members of the committee, from whom I have learned so much. AAUP executive director Julie Schmid has been an indomitable supporter of academic freedom; I am grateful for her helpful reading of a penultimate draft. My Committee A colleague Joan Wallach Scott read the entire book in early draft, chapter by chapter. Her keen critical eye saved me from several mistakes and helped me clarify my ideas. Hans-Joerg Tiede, whose encyclopedic knowledge of AAUP history and policies is unsurpassed, steered me toward important references. Individual chapters were read by Mark Aaronson, Steven Lubet, Michael Meranze, and Mark Simons, all of whom offered useful suggestions. Matthew Finkin and Robert Post's 2009 introduction to concepts of academic freedom in *For the Common Good* provided both a useful model and a helpful guide to handling key issues, especially in the first four chapters. I am extremely fortunate to have Greg Britton as my editor at Johns Hopkins University Press. He encouraged and supported this project from the moment I suggested it. Finally, my wife and life partner, Susan Hutcher, read the entire manuscript and provided more than hortatory encouragement. As ever, she makes it all possible.

Acknowledgments

Notes

Introduction

1. Colleen Flaherty, "Pro-Antifa Professor Out in Iowa," *Inside Higher Ed*, Aug. 26, 2019; Colleen Flaherty, "When a 'Threat' Derails a Career," *Inside Higher Ed*, Feb. 17, 2020; AAUP, "Academic Freedom Case at Emory Law School Resolved," Mar. 16, 2020, https://www.aaup.org/news/academic-freedom-case-emory-law-school-resolved#.XvtoMKZ7lAg; Hank Reichman, "Justice Delayed, Justice Denied," *Academeblog*, Jan. 21, 2020; "Academic Freedom and Tenure: Pacific Lutheran University (Washington)," *Academe: AAUP Bulletin*, 106 (2020), 2-9; Lexi Lonas, "Professor plans to sue Catholic University for firing him over tweets criticizing powerful Democrats," *College Fix*, June 25, 2020; Hank Reichman, "Turning Point Weighs In on the Crisis," *Academeblog*, Mar. 24, 2020, and "Anti-Faculty Coup at National University," *Academeblog*, July 23, 2020.
2. John Dewey, "Academic Freedom," *Educational Review*, 23 (1902), 3, 1.
3. Louis Menand, "The Limits of Academic Freedom," in *The Future of Academic Freedom*, ed. Louis Menand (Chicago: University of Chicago Press, 1996), 5.
4. "Academic Freedom and Tenure in the Quest for National Security: Report of a Special Committee of the American Association of University Professors," *AAUP Bulletin*, 42 (1956), 54-55.

Chapter 1. History

1. J. McKeen Cattell, *University Control* (New York: Science Press, 2013; repr. London: Forgotten Books, 2015).
2. Walter Metzger, *Academic Freedom in the Age of the University* (New York: Columbia University Press, 1955), 89.

3. "1915 Declaration of Principles on Academic Freedom and Academic Tenure," in AAUP, *Policy Documents and Reports*, 11th ed. (Baltimore: Johns Hopkins University Press, 2015), 3-12; Hans-Joerg Tiede, *University Reform: The Founding of the American Association of University Professors* (Baltimore: Johns Hopkins University Press, 2015), 114.

4. Matthew W. Finkin and Robert C. Post, *For the Common Good: Principles of American Academic Freedom* (New Haven, CT: Yale University Press, 2009), 42.

5. Luke Sheahan, "Guardians of the Word: Kirk, Buckley, and the Conservative Struggle with Academic Freedom," *Humanitas*, 25, 1-2 (2012), 44-65.

6. Metzger, *Academic Freedom in the Age of the University*, 218.

7. "1940 Statement of Principles on Academic Freedom and Tenure with 1970 Interpretive Comments," *Policy Documents and Reports*, 13-19.

8. "Policies on Academic Freedom, Dismissal for Cause, Financial Exigency, and Program Discontinuance," *Academe: AAUP Bulletin*, 106 (2020), 50-65.

9. Joy Ann Williamson-Lott, *Jim Crow Campus: Higher Education and the Struggle for a New Southern Social Order* (New York: Teachers College Press, 2019), 51.

10. "Academic Freedom in Mississippi: A Report of a Special Committee," *AAUP Bulletin*, 51 (1965), 341-56.

11. "Affirmative Action in Higher Education: A Report by the Council Commission on Discrimination," *AAUP Bulletin*, 59 (1973), 178-83.

12. "Joint Statement on the Rights and Freedoms of Students," *Policy Documents and Reports*, 381-86.

13. "Academic Freedom and Tenure: Rollins College Report," *Bulletin of the American Association of University Professors*, 19, no. 7 (1933), 416-39. For more on the Rollins College case, see chapter 4.

14. "Statement on Government of Colleges and Universities," *Policy Documents and Reports*, 117-22.

15. "Recommended Institutional Regulations on Academic Freedom and Tenure," *Policy Documents and Reports*, 79-90.

16. Timothy Reese Cain, "Collective Bargaining and Committee A: Five Decades of Unionism and Academic Freedom," *Review of Higher Education*, 44, no. 1 (2020), 57-85. On the AAUP and unionism see Henry Reichman, *The Future of Academic Freedom* (Baltimore: Johns Hopkins University Press, 2019), 223-42.

17. "Joint Statement on Faculty Status of College and University Librarians," *Policy Documents and Reports*, 210-11.

18. Kevin Birmingham, "The Great Shame of Our Profession," *Chronicle of Higher Education*, Feb. 12, 2017.

19. "Recommended Institutional Regulations on Academic Freedom and Tenure (2018 Revision)," *Academe: AAUP Bulletin*, 104 (2018), 23n14.

Chapter 2. Research

1. Matthew W. Finkin and Robert C. Post, *For the Common Good: Principles of American Academic Freedom* (New Haven, CT: Yale University Press, 2009), 55.

2. Finkin and Post, *For the Common Good*, 62-69, discusses the case at length.

3. Robin Wilson, "An Ill-Fated Sex Survey," *Chronicle of Higher Education*, Aug. 2, 2002.

4. "Arming the Past: An Interview with Michael Bellesiles," *Contingent Magazine*, Aug. 24, 2019.

5. John Ross, "Are corporate overreach and political correctness really undermining academic freedom?," *Times Higher Education*, Oct. 15, 2020; "The Sagan Standard: Extraordinary Claims Require Extraordinary Evidence," *Effectiviology*, https://effectiviology.com/sagan-standard-extraordinary-claims-require-extraordinary-evidence/.

6. Zachary Schrag, "Outsourcing Ethics," review of Sarah Babb, *Regulating Human Research: IRBs from Peer Review to Compliance Bureaucracy*, *Academe*, 106, no. 4 (2020), 55-58.

7. Holly Fernandez Lynch, "A New Day for Oversight of Human Subjects Research," *Health Affairs*, Feb. 6, 2017; Louis M Kyriakoudes and Kristine McCusker, "Institutional Review Boards and Oral History: An Update," *Oral History Association*, Jul. 6, 2018.

8. Kate Brown, "The Big Secret in the Academy Is that Most Research Is Secret," *Academe*, 106, no. 2 (2020), 16.

9. Rory Truex, "What the Fear of China Is Doing to American Science," *The Atlantic*, Feb. 16, 2021; "National Security, the Assault on Science, and Academic Freedom," *Academe: AAUP Bulletin*, 104 (2018), 25-37.

10. JASON, "Fundamental Research Security," JSR-19-2I, Dec. 2019, 39-41.

11. "On Partnerships with Foreign Governments: The Case of Confucius Institutes," June 2014, https://www.aaup.org/file/Confucius_Institutes_0.pdf; Naima Green-Riley, "The State Department labeled China's

Confucius programs a bad influence on U.S. students," *Washington Post*, Aug. 25, 2020. The Trump administration's hostility was reaffirmed in Congressional testimony by President Biden's nominee for CIA director, Nicholas Burns, who termed the Confucius Institutes "a genuine risk." Olivier Knox,"Biden's CIA director pick takes aim at China," *Washington Post*, Feb. 25, 2021.

12. C. Wright Mills, *White Collar: The American Middle Classes* (New York: Oxford University Press, 1951), 133–36.

13. *Recommended Principles to Guide Academy-Industry Relationships* (Urbana-Champaign, IL: AAUP, 2014), 43, 29; Sheila Slaughter, "Academic Freedom, Professional Autonomy, and the State," in *The American Academic Profession: Transformation in Contemporary Higher Education*, ed. Joseph C. Hermanowicz (Baltimore: Johns Hopkins University Press, 2011), 51.

14. AAUP, *Recommended Principles*, 47–50.

15. "Statement on Copyright," AAUP, *Policy Documents and Reports*, 11th ed. (Baltimore: Johns Hopkins University Press, 2015), 264–66; Jacob H. Rooksby, *The Branding of the American Mind: How Universities Capture, Manage, and Monetize Intellectual Property and Why It Matters* (Baltimore: Johns Hopkins University Press, 2016), 9; AAUP, *Recommended Principles*, 54.

16. Jeffrey Beall, "What the Open-Access Movement Doesn't Want You to Know," *Academe* 101, no. 3 (2015), 37–40. The UC policy is at https://osc.universityofcalifornia.edu/scholarly-publishing/uc-open-access-policies-background/systemwide-senate/.

17. For more on donor impact on academic freedom, see Henry Reichman, *The Future of Academic Freedom* (Baltimore: Johns Hopkins University Press, 2019), 105–35, from which, unless otherwise cited, quotes in this and the following five paragraphs come.

18. Another example of such a center is the Hoover Institution, located within but not entirely part of Stanford University. See Hank Reichman, "Scott Atlas, Stanford, and the Problem of the Hoover Institution," *Academeblog*, Nov. 19, 2020.

19. Jane Mayer, "Ivanka Trump and Charles Koch Fuel a Cancel-Culture Clash at Wichita State," *New Yorker*, June 11, 2020.

20. Tim Schwab, "Playing Games with Public Health Data," *Nation*, Dec. 14-21, 2020, 24–31.

21. Climate Science Legal Defense Fund, "Research Protections in State Open Records Laws: An Analysis and Ranking," 2d ed., 2019.

22. "Academic Freedom and Tenure: Louisiana State University, Baton Rouge," *Academe: AAUP Bulletin*, 97 (2011), 21–50.

23. Reference is to Yale law professor Stephen Carter, who is a novelist; Princeton historian Nell Irvin Painter, who took up painting; and Cal Tech mathematician Phil Alvin, of the punk rock group the Blasters, who still performs and records with his brother Dave.

24. Finkin and Post, *For the Common Good*, 73-77.

25. "Academic Freedom and Artistic Expression," *Policy Documents and Reports*, 40-41.

Chapter 3. Teaching

1. Matthew W. Finkin and Robert C. Post, *For the Common Good: Principles of American Academic Freedom* (New Haven, CT: Yale University Press, 2009), 81.

2. "Freedom in the Classroom," AAUP, *Policy Documents and Reports*, 11th ed. (Baltimore: Johns Hopkins University Press, 2015), 20-27.

3. "Academic Freedom and Tenure: Adelphi University," *AAUP Bulletin*, 53 (1965), 283-84. See also Finkin and Post, *For the Common Good*, 84-86.

4. Finkin and Post, *For the Common Good*, 103-4.

5. "Does College Turn People into Liberals?," *Conversation*, Feb. 2, 2018; Neil Gross, "The indoctrination myth," *New York Times*, Mar. 3, 2012.

6. "Charles Koch Foundation raises concern over call to intimidate scholars as courses move online amid COVID-19 pandemic," https://www.charleskochfoundation.org/news/ckf-raises-concern -call-intimidate-scholars-courses-online-covid-pandemic/. Koch's donor network provides much of Turning Point's funding, however.

7. "Statement on Professional Ethics," *Policy Documents and Reports*, 145-46.

8. "The History, Uses, and Abuses of Title IX," *Academe: AAUP Bulletin*, 102 (2016), 69-99.

9. Patricia A. Adler and Peter Adler, "Administrative Interference and Overreach: The 'Adler Controversy' and the Twenty-First-Century University," in *Challenges to Academic Freedom*, ed. Joseph C. Hermanowicz (Baltimore: Johns Hopkins University Press, 2021), 25-45.

10. "Academic Freedom and Tenure: Louisiana State University, Baton Rouge: Supplementary Report on a Censured Administration," *Academe: AAUP Bulletin*, 102 (2016), 6.

11. "Faculty respond to professor's use of N-word by calling for institutional change around racial justice," *Augsburg Echo*, Nov. 30, 2018.

12. Shannon Dea, "Academic Freedom and the N-word," *University Affairs/Affaires Universitaires*, Aug. 21, 2020.

13. Suzanne Nossel, *Dare to Speak: Defending Free Speech for All* (New York: Dey Street, 2020), 83.

14. The American University resolution is at https://www.american.edu /facultysenate/upload/Faculty-senate-minutes-4-4-18-final.pdf. For more on diversity see Henry Reichman, "Academic Freedom and the Challenge of Diversity: Upholding Two Core Values Essential to the Pursuit of the Common Good," *Liberal Education*, 106, no. 3 (2020), 40-45.

15. "Academic Freedom and Tenure: The Ohio State University," *AAUP Bulletin*, 58 (1972), 306-21.

16. "Academic Freedom and Tenure: Evansville College," *AAUP Bulletin*, 35 (1949), 91-92.

17. Tom Bartlett, "'Scared to Death to Teach': Internal Report Cites 'Chilling Effect,'" *Chronicle of Higher Education*, Sep. 21, 2020.

18. Finkin and Post, *For the Common Good*, 92.

19. John K. Wilson, "Academic Freedom and Classroom Conduct," *Academeblog*, Feb. 12, 2021.

20. "The Freedom to Teach," *Policy Documents and Reports*, 28.

21. Carla Rivera, "Reprimand of Cal State Fullerton math professor in textbook dispute stands," *Los Angeles Times*, Nov. 5, 2015.

22. "Academic Freedom and Tenure: Benedict College (South Carolina): A Supplementary Report on a Censured Administration," *Academe: AAUP Bulletin*, 91 (2005), 51-54; "Academic Freedom and Tenure: Nicholls State University (Louisiana)," *Academe: AAUP Bulletin*, 94 (2008), 60-69.

23. "Academic Freedom and Tenure: Louisiana State University, Baton Rouge," *Academe: AAUP Bulletin*, 97 (2011), 41-50.

24. "Statement on Teaching Evaluation" and "Observations on the Association's Statement on Teaching Evaluation," *Policy Documents and Reports*, 219-26.

25. John W. Lawrence, "Student Evaluations of Teaching Are Not Valid," *Academe*, 104, no. 3 (2018); Hank Reichman, "Justice Delayed, Justice

Denied," *Academeblog*, Jan. 21, 2020; Jason Rodriguez, "The Weaponization of Student Evaluations of Teaching: Bullying and the Undermining of Academic Freedom," *Journal of Academic Freedom*, 10 (2019).

26. Richard Hofstadter, *Anti-Intellectualism in American Life* (New York: Random House, 1962), 339. See also Erik Gilbert, "An Insider's Take on Assessment: It May Be Worse Than You Thought," *Chronicle of Higher Education*, Jan. 12, 2018.

27. "Mandated Assessment of Educational Outcomes," *Policy Documents and Reports*, 245-53.

28. This section summarizes arguments made in Henry Reichman, *The Future of Academic Freedom* (Baltimore: Johns Hopkins University Press, 2019), 69-73.

29. Jonathan Poritz and Jonathan Rees, "Academic Freedom in Online Education," *Academe*, 107, no. 1 (2021), 14.

30. National Coalition against Censorship, "Zoom, Facebook, and YouTube Threaten Academic Freedom," *Academeblog*, Oct. 8, 2020; University of California Academic Senate Committee on Academic Freedom, "Censorship By Zoom And Other Private Platforms," *Academeblog*, Feb. 5, 2021; Poritz and Rees, "Academic Freedom in Online Education," 11-14.

31. "Statement on Intellectual Property," *Policy Documents and Reports*, 261-63.

32. "Academic Freedom at Religiously Affiliated Institutions: The 'Limitations' Clause in the 1940 *Statement of Principles on Academic Freedom and Tenure*," *Policy Documents and Reports*, 64-67.

33. "Academic Freedom and Tenure: The Catholic University of America," *Academe: AAUP Bulletin*, 75 (1989), 27-40.

34. Colleen Flaherty, "Faith and Freedom," *Inside Higher Ed*, Jan. 14, 2016.

35. Hofstadter, *Anti-Intellectualism in American Life*, 134.

36. Reichman, *Future of Academic Freedom*, 190-91. For more on Liberty University, see John K. Wilson, "Attacking Liberty at Liberty," *Academeblog*, Apr. 15, 2020, and Calum Best, "The Falkirk Center: Liberty University's Slime Factory," *Bulwark*, Jan. 15, 2021.

Chapter 4. Citizenship

1. Walter Metzger, "Essay II," in *Freedom and Order in the University*, ed. Samuel Gorovitz (Cleveland: Press of Western Reserve University,

1967), 70; Matthew W. Finkin and Robert C. Post, *For the Common Good: Principles of American Academic Freedom*, (New Haven, CT: Yale University Press, 2009), 127.

2. Arthur O. Lovejoy, "Academic Freedom," in *Encyclopedia of the Social Sciences*, vol. 1, ed. Edwin R. A. Seligman and Alvin Johnson (London: Macmillan, 1930), 386; David Bromwich, "Academic Freedom and Its Opponents," in *Who's Afraid of Academic Freedom?*, ed. Akeel Bilgrami and Jonathan Cole (New York: Columbia University Press, 2015), 27; Judith Butler, "The Criminalization of Knowledge," *Chronicle of Higher Education*, May 27, 2018; Erwin Chemerinsky and Howard Gillman, *Free Speech on Campus* (New Haven, CT: Yale University Press, 2017).

3. Finkin and Post, *For the Common Good*, 140.

4. Arthur Lovejoy and John Wigmore, "Academic Freedom: Professor Lovejoy's Criticism of Professor Wigmore's Proposals and the Latter's Reply," *Nation*, 103 (1916), 561-62. For more on this debate, see Hans-Joerg Tiede, *University Reform: The Founding of the American Association of University Professors* (Baltimore: Johns Hopkins University Press, 2015), 118-20.

5. Keith Whittington, "Academic Freedom and the Scope of Protections for Extramural Speech," *Academe*, 105, no. 1 (2019), 23-24.

6. "Statement of Principles, 1938," *AAUP Bulletin*, 25 (1939), 27.

7. "Academic Freedom and Tenure: University of Illinois," *AAUP Bulletin*, 49 (1963), 25-43. For an engaging account of the Koch case in the context of the larger history of the 1960s, see Matthew C. Erlich, *Dangerous Ideas at the University of Illinois: Sex, Conspiracy, and Academic Freedom in the Age of JFK* (Urbana, IL: University of Illinois Press, 2021).

8. David Fellman, "Report of Committee A, 1963-1964," *AAUP Bulletin*, 50 (1964), 125-35.

9. "Committee A Statement on Extramural Utterances," AAUP, *Policy Documents and Reports*, 11th ed. (Baltimore: Johns Hopkins University Press, 2015), 31.

10. "Academic Freedom and Tenure in the Quest for National Security," *AAUP Bulletin*, 42, no. 1 (1956), 58, 70.

11. "Academic Freedom and Tenure: The University of California at Los Angeles," *AAUP Bulletin*, 57 (1971), 398-99.

12. Scott Jaschik, "A Holocaust Denier Resurfaces," *Inside Higher Ed*, Feb. 8, 2006.

13. Keith Whittington, "Academic Freedom, Even for Amy Wax," *Academeblog*, July 28, 2019.

14. Elizabeth Redden, "UW Milwaukee Calls Lecturer's Comments on Vanessa Guillen 'Repugnant,'" *Inside Higher Ed*, July 6, 2020.

15. Henry Reichman, *The Future of Academic Freedom* (Baltimore: Johns Hopkins University Press, 2019), 2, 79. For a survey of such incidents, see 74-90.

16. Lexi Lonas, "Professor plans to sue Catholic University for firing him over tweets criticizing powerful Democrats," *College Fix*, June 25, 2020.

17. "Academic Freedom and Electronic Communications," *Policy Documents and Reports*, 42.

18. AAUP, AACU, AFT, "Taking a Stand against Harassment, Part of the Broader Threat to Higher Education," Sept. 7, 2017.

19. Reichman, *Future of Academic Freedom*, 64-65.

20. "Academic Freedom and Tenure: The University of Illinois at Urbana-Champaign," *Academe: AAUP Bulletin*, 101 (2015), 27-47. I chaired this investigation and participated in writing the report.

21. Michael Meranze, "The Order of Civility," *Remaking the University*, Sept. 7, 2014.

22. Kenneth S. Stern, *The Conflict over the Conflict: The Israel/Palestine Campus Debate* (Toronto: New Jewish Press, 2020), 75, 124.

23. "The AAUP Opposes Academic Boycotts," *Academe*, 91, no. 4 (2005), 57; "On Academic Boycotts," *Academe*, 92, no. 5 (2006), 42. See also Henry Reichman, "Against Academic Boycotts," *Inside Higher Ed*, Dec. 12, 2013, and "Why the AAUP Opposes Both Boycotts and Restrictions on Their Supporters," *Inside Higher Ed*, Aug. 8, 2018.

24. "AAUP Statement on Academic Boycotts," May 10, 2013; AAUP, "Open Letter to Members of the American Studies Association," Dec. 6, 2013; AAUP, "Statement on Anti-Boycott Legislation," Feb. 4, 2014; AAUP, "Statement on Anti-BDS Legislation and Universities," Aug. 8, 2018; and Hank Reichman, "Anti-BDS Law Challenged at Texas Universities," *Academeblog*, Dec. 19, 2018. For more on such legislation, see PEN America, *Wrong Answer: How Good Faith Attempts to Address Free Speech and Anti-Semitism on Campus Could Backfire* (New York: PEN America, 2017).

25. "Statement on Anti-Boycott Legislation," Feb. 4, 2014.

26. Hank Reichman, "And Now There's a Blacklist?" *Academeblog*, Sept. 10, 2014, and "Another Blacklist Emerges," *Academeblog*, Aug. 1, 2016. On Canary Mission, see also Stern, *The Conflict over the Conflict*, 125-27.

27. Elizabeth Redden, "The Right to a Recommendation?," *Inside Higher Ed*, Sept. 19, 2018; "Standing with John Cheney-Lippold," *Academeblog*, Sept. 19, 2018; Hank Reichman, "Standing with Professional Ethics," *Academeblog*, Sept. 20, 2018, and "Addendum to 'Standing with Professional Ethics,'" *Academeblog*, Sept. 21, 2018; AAUP, "A Statement of the Association's Council: Freedom and Responsibility," *AAUP Bulletin*, 56 (1970), 375-76.

28. Steven Lubet, "The Dean of BDS," *Bulwark*, June 29, 2020; John K. Wilson, "In Defense of Ilana Feldman and BDS Supporters," *Academeblog*, June 20, 2020.

29. Hank Reichman, "Are Academic Administrators Entitled to Academic Freedom?," *Academeblog*, Nov. 28, 2018.

30. C. Wright Mills, *White Collar: The American Middle Classes* (New York: Oxford University Press, 1951), 136.

31. Sidney Hook, "Academic Freedom and 'The Trojan Horse' in American Education," *Bulletin of the American Association of University Professors*, 25, no. 5 (1939), 550-55.

32. "Academic Freedom in the Quest for National Security," *AAUP Bulletin*, 42 (1956), 58.

33. "Statement on Professors and Political Activity," *Policy Documents and Reports*, 39.

34. Christopher Edley, Jr., "The Torture Memos and Academic Freedom," Apr. 10, 2008, https://www.law.berkeley.edu/article/the-torture -memos-and-academic-freedom/; Colleen Flaherty, "Stanford Senate Speaks Out against Scott Atlas," *Inside Higher Ed*, Nov. 23, 2020; Hank Reichman, "Scott Atlas, Stanford, and the Problem of the Hoover Institution," *Academeblog*, Nov. 19, 2020; Camille G. Caldera and Michelle G. Kurilla, "Open Letter Calls on Harvard to Develop 'Accountability Guidelines' on Hiring Former Trump Administration Officials," *Harvard Crimson*, Nov. 19, 2020.

35. Finkin and Post, *For the Common Good*, 113.

36. "On the Relationship of Faculty Governance to Academic Freedom," *Policy Documents and Reports*, 123-25.

37. "Academic Freedom and Tenure: Rollins College Report," *Bulletin of the American Association of University Professors*, 19, no. 7 (1933), 416-39.

38. "Recommended Institutional Regulations on Academic Freedom and Tenure (2018 Revision)," *Academe: AAUP Bulletin*, 104 (2018), 23n14.

39. "Academic Freedom and Tenure: Community College of Aurora (Colorado)," *Academe: AAUP Bulletin*, 103 (2017), 9.

Chapter 5. Tenure

1. The following discussion and defense of tenure is based largely on Fritz Machlup, "In Defense of Academic Tenure," *AAUP Bulletin*, 50 (1964), 112-24; William Van Alstyne, "Tenure: A Summary, Explanation, and 'Defense,'" *AAUP Bulletin*, 57 (1971), 328-33; and Ralph S. Brown and Jordan E. Kurland, "Academic Tenure and Academic Freedom," *Law and Contemporary Problems*, 53, no. 3, Freedom and Tenure in the Academy: The Fiftieth Anniversary of the 1940 Statement of Principles (1990), 325-55.

2. Commission on Academic Tenure in Higher Education, *Faculty Tenure: A Report and Recommendations* (San Francisco: Jossey-Bass, 1973).

3. Matthew W. Finkin, "'A Higher Order of Liberty in the Workplace': Academic Freedom and Tenure in the Vortex of Employment Practices and Law," *Law and Contemporary Problems*, 53, no. 3 (1990), 366.

4. Van Alstyne, "Tenure," 329.

5. Clark Byse and Louis Joughin, *Tenure in American Higher Education: Plans, Practices, and the Law* (Ithaca, NY: Cornell University Press, 1959), 4.

6. "Ensuring Academic Freedom in Politically Controversial Academic Personnel Decisions," *Academe: AAUP Bulletin*, 97 (2011), 97.

7. Machlup, "In Defense of Academic Tenure," 115.

8. Adrianna Kezar, Tom DePaola, and Daniel T. Scott, *The Gig Academy: Mapping Labor in the Neoliberal University* (Baltimore: Johns Hopkins University Press, 2019), 45, 51, 56.

9. Quoted in Brown and Kurland, "Academic Tenure and Academic Freedom," 347.

10. "Recommended Institutional Regulations," AAUP, *Policy Documents and Reports*, 11th ed. (Baltimore: Johns Hopkins University Press, 2015), 81.

11. "The Role of the Faculty in Conditions of Financial Exigency," *Academe: AAUP Bulletin*, 99 (2013), 118-47. An abridged version is in *Policy Documents and Reports*, 292-308.

12. "Academic Freedom and Tenure: City University of New York: Mass Dismissals under Financial Exigency," *AAUP Bulletin*, 63, no. 2 (1977), 60-81.

13. "Academic Freedom and Tenure: San Diego State University: An Administration's Response to Fiscal Stress," *Academe,* 79 no. 2 (1993), 94-116.

14. "Academic Freedom and Tenure: National Louis University (Illinois)," *Academe: AAUP Bulletin*, 99 (2013), 17-29.

15. Michael Bérubé, "Some Exigent Words about Financial Exigency," *Academe* (online only), 106, no. 2 (2020).

16. Shawn Hubler, "Colleges slash budgets in the pandemic, with 'nothing off-limits,'" *New York Times*, Oct. 26, 2020; Dan Baumann, "A Brutal Tally: Higher Ed Lost 650,000 Jobs Last Year," *Chronicle of Higher Education*, Feb. 5, 2021; Emma Pettit, "Covid-19 Cuts Hit Contingent Faculty Hard," *Chronicle of Higher Education*, Oct. 26, 2020. As this book neared completion, the AAUP undertook an omnibus investigation of shared governance violations at eight institutions where layoffs of faculty had been imposed in response to the pandemic. The investigation was also empowered to look into other enrollment and financial challenges facing many institutions, and the impact of these challenges on higher education, especially the humanities and liberal arts, and on academic freedom. The author is a member of the investigating committee.

17. "Statement from Medaille College, Office of the President," Apr. 15, 2020.

18. Machlup, "In Defense of Academic Tenure," 116.

19. Brown and Kurland, "Academic Tenure and Academic Freedom," 342-43; "Post-Tenure Review: An AAUP Response," *Policy Documents and Reports*, 229-34.

20. Caitlin Rosenthal, "Fundamental Freedom or Fringe Benefit? Rice University and the Administrative History of Tenure, 1935-1963," *Journal of Academic Freedom*, 2 (2011).

21. Material in this section is excerpted with permission from Henry Reichman, "Do Adjuncts Have Academic Freedom? or, Why Tenure Matters," *Academe*, 107, no. 1 (2021).

22. Kezar, DePaola, and Scott, *Gig Academy*, 37, 34.

23. Jan Clausen and Eva-Maria Swidler, "Academic Freedom from Below: Toward an Adjunct-Centered Struggle," *Journal of Academic Freedom*, 4 (2013); Stephen P. Mumme, with Marki LeCompte, Caprice Lawless, Myron Hulen, Don Eron, William Timpson, and Nathanial Bork, "Instructor Impermanence and the Need for Community College Adjunct Faculty Reform in Colorado," *Academic Labor: Research and Artistry*, 2, art. 9 (2018).

24. Ernst Benjamin, "The Eroding Foundations of Academic Freedom and Professional Integrity: Implications of the Diminishing Proportion of Tenured Faculty for Organizational Effectiveness in Higher Education," *Journal of Academic Freedom*, 1 (2010); Michael Bérubé and Jennifer Ruth, *The Humanities, Higher Education, and Academic Freedom: Three Necessary Arguments* (New York: Palgrave Macmillan, 2015), 87.

25. Clausen and Swidler, "Academic Freedom from Below."

26. John Warner, "19 Theses on Tenure," *Inside Higher Ed*, Feb. 21, 2017.

Chapter 6. Law

1. Louis Menand, *The Metaphysical Club: A Story of Ideas in America* (New York: Farrar, Straus, Giroux, 2001), 238-43, 417.

2. Ellen Schrecker, *No Ivory Tower: McCarthyism and the Universities* (New York: Oxford University Press, 1986); Richard Hofstadter, *Anti-Intellectualism in American Life* (New York: Random House, 1962), 41.

3. "Academic Freedom and Tenure in the Quest for National Security: Report of a Special Committee of the American Association of University Professors," *AAUP Bulletin*, 42, no. 1 (1956), 49-107.

4. *Adler v. Board of Education*, 342 U.S. 485 (1952). William W. Van Alstyne, "Academic Freedom and the First Amendment in the Supreme Court of the United States: An Unhurried Historical Review," *Law and Contemporary Problems*, 53, no. 3, Freedom and Tenure in the Academy: The Fiftieth Anniversary of the 1940 Statement of Principles (1990), 107. On *Adler*, see Marjorie Heins, *Priests of Our Democracy: The Supreme Court, Academic Freedom, and the Anti-Communist Purge* (New York: NYU Press, 2013), 119-22.

5. On the four 1957 cases, see Heins, *Priests of Our Democracy*, 177-82. The other cases involved a narrowing of the 1940 anti-Communist Smith Act, invalidating procedures of a federal loyalty program that

resulted in dismissal of a career diplomat, and reversing a contempt conviction of a labor organizer who refused to answer questions posed by the House Un-American Activities Committee.

6. *Sweezy v. New Hampshire*, 354 U.S. 234 (1957), 250, 261-63.

7. *Keyishian v. Board of Regents*, 385 U.S. 589 (1967), 602-3, quoting in part *Shelton v. Tucker*, 364 U.S. 479, 487 (1960) and *United States v. Associated Press*, 52 F.Supp. 362, 372 (D.D.C. 1945). On *Keyishian*, see Heins, *Priests of Our Democracy*, 193-222.

8. William A. Kaplin and Barbara A. Lee, *The Law of Higher Education*, 3rd ed. (San Francisco: Jossey-Bass, 1995), 301. See also Walter P. Metzger, "Profession and Constitution: Two Definitions of Academic Freedom in America," *Texas Law Review*, 66 (1987-88), 1265-1308.

9. *Epperson v. Arkansas*, 393 U.S. 97 (1968), 113-14.

10. *Board of Regents v. Roth*, 408 U.S. 564 (1972).

11. Van Alstyne, "Unhurried Review," 132-33.

12. *Cooper v. Ross*, 472 F. Supp. 802 (E.D. Ark. 1979); *Ollman v. Toll*, 518 F. Supp. 1196 (D. Md. 1981), *aff'd*, 704 F. 2d 139 (4th Cir. 1983).

13. Van Alstyne, "Unhurried Review," 138; Matthew Finkin, "On 'Institutional' Academic Freedom," *Texas Law Review*, 61 (1983), 817, 839; "Some Thoughts on the Powell Opinion in Bakke," *Academe* 65, no. 3 (1979), 192.

14. *Regents of the University of Michigan v. Ewing*, 474 U.S. 214 (1985), 226n12.

15. J. Peter Byrne, "Academic Freedom: A 'Special Concern of the First Amendment,'" *Yale Law Journal*, 99 (1989), 312.

16. *Urofsky v. Gilmore*, 216 F.3d (2000) 401, 410, 415, *cert. denied*, 531 U.S. 1070 (2001). See also Byrne, "Constitutional Academic Freedom in Scholarship and in Court," *Chronicle of Higher Education*, Jan. 5, 2001.

17. Lindsay Ellis, "What Is Academic Freedom? Statement That Alarmed Professors at U. of Texas Sets Off Debate," *Chronicle of Higher Education*, July 24, 2018.

18. *Minnesota State Board for Community Colleges v. Knight*, 465 U.S. 271 (1984), 287-88, 296-97.

19. Robert A. Gorman, "The Yeshiva Decision," *Academe*, 66, no. 4 (1980), 188-97, which includes both the majority and dissenting opinions.

20. *Pickering v. Board of Education*, 391 U.S. 563 (1968).

21. "Protecting an Independent Faculty Voice: Academic Freedom after *Garcetti v. Ceballos*," *Academe*, 95, no. 6 (2009), 75-76. The report's

executive summary is in AAUP, *Policy Documents and Reports*, 11th ed. (Baltimore: Johns Hopkins University Press, 2015), 126-29.

22. Kaplin and Lee, *Law of Higher Education*, 199. For an example of how the public interest standard can imperil academic freedom, see the case of the LSU professor charged with sexual harassment for classroom speech discussed in chapter 3.

23. *Garcetti v. Ceballos*, 547 U.S. 410 (2006), 425.

24. *Hong v. Grant*, 516 F. Supp. 2d 1158 (C.D. Cal. 2007).

25. *Renken v. Gregory*, 541 F. 3d. 769 (7th Cir. 2008); *Payne v. University of Arkansas Fort Smith*, 2006 U.S. Dist. LEXIS 52806 (W.D. Ark. Jul. 26, 2006); *Nichols v. Univ. of S. Miss.* 669 f. Supp. 2d 684, 698-99 (S.D. Miss. 2009); *Miller v. Univ. of S. Ala.*, No. 09-0146-KD-B, 2010 U.S. Dist. LEXIS 48643 (S.D. Ala. May 17, 2010).

26. *Adams v. Trustees of the University of North Carolina–Wilmington*, 640 F. 3d 550 (4th Cir., 2011); *Demers v. Austin*, 746 F.3d 402 (9th Cir. Wash. Jan. 29, 2014).

27. Quoted in Henry Reichman, *The Future of Academic Freedom* (Baltimore: Johns Hopkins University Press, 2019), 256-57.

28. *John McAdams v. Marquette University*, 2018 WI 88, July 6, 2018, Majority Opinion, 63n35, 48, 58. For more on the case see Reichman, *Future of Academic Freedom*, 90-102.

29. Philip Lee, "A Contract Theory of Academic Freedom," *Saint Louis University Law Journal* 59 (2015).

30. Ralph S. Brown and Jordan E. Kurland, "Academic Tenure and Academic Freedom," *Law and Contemporary Problems*, 53, no. 3, Freedom and Tenure in the Academy: The Fiftieth Anniversary of the 1940 Statement of Principles (1990)," 335-40.

31. *Greene v. Howard University*, 412 F2d 1135 (DC Cir 1969); *Perry v. Sindermann*, 408 U.S. 601 (1972). See also Matthew W. Finkin, "'A Higher Order of Liberty in the Workplace': Academic Freedom and Tenure in the Vortex of Employment Practices and Law," *Law and Contemporary Problems*, 53, no. 3 (1990), 360-63.

32. "Faculty Handbooks as Enforceable Contracts: A State Guide," https://www.aaup.org/our-programs/legal-program/faculty-handbooks-guide.

33. Byrne, "Academic Freedom: A 'Special Concern of the First Amendment,'" 251.

34. Rachel Levinson-Waldman, "Review of Robert Post, *Democracy, Expertise, and Academic Freedom*," *Tulsa Law Review*, 48, no. 2 (2012), 245.

Chapter 7. Students

1. "Academic Freedom at the University of Pittsburgh," *Bulletin of the American Association of University Professors* 15, no. 8 (Dec. 1929), 380–81; Ralph S. Fuchs, "Academic Freedom—Its Basic Philosophy, Function, and History," *Law and Contemporary Problems*, 28 (1963), 432.

2. Walter P. Metzger, "Profession and Constitution: Two Definitions of Academic Freedom in America," *Texas Law Review*, 66 (1988), 1270, quoted in Matthew W. Finkin and Robert C. Post, *For the Common Good: Principles of American Academic Freedom* (New Haven, CT: Yale University Press, 2009), 219–20n1.

3. Robert Cohen, *When the Old Left Was Young: Student Radicals and America's First Mass Student Movement, 1929–1941* (New York: Oxford University Press, 1993).

4. Joy Ann Williamson-Lott, *Jim Crow Campus: Higher Education and the Struggle for a New Southern Social Order* (New York: Teachers College Press, 2019), 46.

5. Erwin Chemerinsky and Howard Gillman, *Free Speech on Campus* (New Haven, CT: Yale University Press, 2017), 74–76; Reginald E. Zelnik, "On the Side of the Angels: The Berkeley Faculty and the FSM," in *The Free Speech Movement: Reflections on Berkeley in the 1960s*, ed. Robert Cohen and Zelnik (Berkeley: University of California Press, 2002), 270, 324.

6. Robert Cohen, "This Was *Their* Fight and *They* Had to Fight It: The FSM's Nonradical Rank and File," in Cohen and Zelnik, *The Free Speech Movement*, 228.

7. On Black student activism, see Ibram X. Kendi, *The Black Campus Movement: Black Students and the Racial Reconstitution of Higher Education, 1965–1972* (New York: Palgrave Macmillan, 2012). and Stefan M. Bradley, *Upending the Ivory Tower: Civil Rights, Black Power, and the Ivy League* (New York: NYU Press, 2018).

8. On the Nixon Commission, see Roderick A. Ferguson, *We Demand: The University and Student Protests* (Berkeley: University of California Press, 2017), 16–24.

9. *Dixon v. Alabama*, 294 F.2d 150 (5th Cir. 1961).

10. William W. Van Alstyne, "Academic Freedom and the First Amendment in the Supreme Court of the United States: An Unhurried

Historical Review," *Law and Contemporary Problems*, 53, no. 3, Freedom and Tenure in the Academy: The Fiftieth Anniversary of the 1940 Statement of Principles (1990), 117.

11. *Tinker v. Des Moines School District*, 393 U.S. 503 (1969).

12. *Healy v. James*, 408 U.S. 169 (1972).

13. Van Alstyne, "Unhurried Review," 125.

14. Metzger, "Profession and Constitution," 1304-5.

15. "A Statement of the Association's Special Committee on Challenge and Change," *AAUP Bulletin,* 55, no. 4 (1969), 461-62.

16. Robert C. Post, "Academic Freedom and the 'Intifada Curriculum,'" *Academe* 89, no. 3 (2003), 19.

17. Alan Wolfe, "A Summer Look at the Spring Events," *AAUP Bulletin*, 56, no. 3 (1970), 269-72.

18. Samuel Krislov, "The Obligation to Reject Engagement," *AAUP Bulletin*, 56, no. 3 (1970), 276-78.

19. Guenter Lewy and Stanley Rothman, "On Student Power," *AAUP Bulletin*, 56, no. 3 (1970), 279-82.

20. *Report of the Committee on Freedom of Expression at Yale*, Dec. 1974. The report has been republished, but without the dissent, as *Campus Speech in Crisis: What the Yale Experience Can Teach America* (New York: Encounter Books, 2016). Robert C. Post, "The Classic First Amendment Tradition Under Stress: Freedom of Speech and the University," in *The Free Speech Century*, Lee C. Bollinger and Geoffrey R. Stone, ed. (New York: Oxford University Press, 2019), 316n81.

21. "Joint Statement on Rights and Freedoms of Students," AAUP, *Policy Documents and Reports*, 11th ed. (Baltimore: Johns Hopkins University Press, 2015), 381-86.

22. "Draft Statement on Student Participation in College and University Government," *AAUP Bulletin*, 56, no. 1 (1970), 33-35.

23. "Threats to the Independence of Student Media," *Academe: AAUP Bulletin*, 103 (2017), 25-33.

24. Post, "Academic Freedom and the 'Intifada Curriculum,'" 16-20.

25. "Academic Freedom and Tenure: University of Nebraska-Lincoln," *Academe: AAUP Bulletin*, 104 (2018), 2-12.

26. "The Rise and Fall of Silent Sam," *Chronicle of Higher Education*, Jan. 17, 2019.

27. "Academic Freedom and Tenure: University of Missouri (Columbia)," *Academe: AAUP Bulletin*, 102 (2016), 25-43.

28. PEN America, "Wrong Answer: How Good Faith Attempts to Address Free Speech and Anti-Semitism on Campus Could Backfire," Nov. 7, 2017; "Campus Free-Speech Legislation: History, Progress, and Problems," *Academe: AAUP Bulletin*, 104 (2018), 38–47.

29. Vimal Patel, "The New 'In Loco Parentis,'" *Chronicle of Higher Education*, Feb. 18, 2019; Peter F. Lake, "The Rise of Duty and the Fall of *In Loco Parentis* and Other Protective Tort Doctrines in Higher Education Law," *Missouri Law Review*, 64, no. 1 (1999), 1–28.

30. Kristen Peters, "Protecting the Millennial College Student," *Review of Law and Social Justice*, 16, 2 (2007), 459.

31. Henry Reichman, *The Future of Academic Freedom* (Baltimore: Johns Hopkins University Press, 2019), 164.

32. "On Freedom of Expression and Campus Speech Codes," *Policy Documents and Reports*, 361–62.

33. Peters, "Protecting the Millennial College Student," 456.

34. Greg Lukianoff, *Unlearning Liberty: Campus Censorship and the End of American Debate* (New York: Encounter, 2012); John Seery, "Somewhere between a Jeremiad and a Eulogy," *Modern Age*, 59, no. 3 (2017). Two troubling cases illustrative of the dangers associated with these trends occurred at Oberlin College in 2016 and Smith College in 2020. See Abraham Socher, "O Oberlin, My Oberlin," *Commentary*, Sept. 2019 and Michael Powell, "Inside a Battle Over Race, Class and Power at Smith College," *New York Times*, Feb. 24, 2021.

35. Jonathan Marks, *Let's Be Reasonable: A Conservative Case for Liberal Education* (Princeton, NJ: Princeton University Press, 2021), 5; Scott Jaschik, "'Campus Uprisings,'" [Interview with editors of *Campus Uprisings: How Student Activists and Collegiate Leaders Resist Racism and Create Hope* (New York: Teachers College Press, 2020)] *Inside Higher Ed*, Jul. 14, 2020.

Chapter 8. Knowledge

1. Bryan Pietsch, "Texas hospital says man, 30, died after attending a 'Covid party,'" *New York Times*, July 12, 2020.

2. "National Security, the Assault on Science, and Academic Freedom," *Academe: AAUP Bulletin*, 104 (2018), 25–37.

3. Jacob Carter, Emily Berman, Anita Desikan, Charise Johnson, and Gretchen Goldman, *The State of Science in the Trump Era: Damage*

Done, Lessons Learned, and a Path to Progress (Union of Concerned Scientists, 2019).

4. Ernst Benjamin, "The March for Science Is Also a March for Academic Freedom," *Academeblog*, April 18, 2017.

5. Robert Post, "Rebellion, Authority, and Knowledge," *Academe*, 106, no. 2 (2020), 12-13.

6. "In Defense of Knowledge and Higher Education," *Academe: AAUP Bulletin*, 106 (2020), 10-14.

7. John Dewey, "Academic Freedom," *Educational Review*, xxiii (1902), 4-6.

8. Aaron Hanlon, "Lies about the Humanities—and the Lying Liars Who Tell Them," *Chronicle of Higher Education*, Dec. 7, 2018.

9. Judith Butler, "A Dissenting View from the Humanities on the AAUP's Statement on Knowledge," *Academe*, 106, no. 2 (2020), 25.

10. Michael Meranze, "For a Reparative University," *Academe*, 106, no. 4 (2020), 31.

11. Post, "Rebellion, Authority, and Knowledge," 14.

12. Joy Connolly, "Dialogue across Divides," *Academe*, 106, no. 2 (2020), 34.

13. Scott Carlson, "When College Was a Public Good," *Chronicle of Higher Education*, Nov. 27, 2016, quoted in "In Defense of Knowledge and Higher Education."

14. Henry Reichman, *The Future of Academic Freedom* (Baltimore: Johns Hopkins University Press, 2019), 11-13; Christopher Newfield, *The Great Mistake: How We Wrecked Public Universities and How We Can Fix Them* (Baltimore: Johns Hopkins University Press, 2016), 278-79, 281.

15. Newfield, *Great Mistake*, 56, 58.

16. Doug Lederman, "The Public's Support for (and Doubts about) Higher Ed," *Inside Higher Ed*, June 17, 2019.

17. American Academy of Arts and Sciences, "The Humanities in American Life: A Survey of the Public's Attitudes and Engagement," Nov. 9, 2020, https://www.amacad.org/humanities-indicators /humanities-american-life-survey-publics-attitudes-and-engagement.

18. Connolly, "Dialogue across Divides," 37.

19. Nicholas Lemann, "The American Way: Richard Hofstadter's *Anti-Intellectualism in American Life* Reviewed," *Columbia Journalism Review*, Sept.-Oct. 2014; Hofstadter, *Anti-Intellectualism in American Life* (New York: Random House, 1962), 34, 217.

20. Lemann, "The American Way."

21. For an oral history of the Sokal affair, see Jennifer Ruark, "Bait and Switch," *Chronicle of Higher Education*, Jan. 1, 2017. On "Sokal Squared," see Hank Reichman, "Links and Random Thoughts on the 'Sokal Squared' Hoax," *Academeblog*, Oct. 8, 2018.

22. Edward Shils, "Do We Still Need Academic Freedom?," *Minerva*, 32, no. 1 (1994), 97-98: "An aggressive and intimidating body of antinomian academic opinion has gained in strength. It has objectives very different from those which the American Association of University Professors once sought to protect. In its view the equality of 'genders,' the equality of 'races,' the equality of 'cultures,' the normality of homosexuality are the only real values, while the criteria of truthfulness are illusory, deceptive, and fundamentally intended to exploit women, people of colour, homosexuals, and the poor. The value of academic freedom is denied; it counts for nothing alongside these other values, since the truth which it would protect is declared to be an illusion."

23. Aaron Hanlon, "Postmodernism didn't cause Trump. It explains him," *Washington Post*, Aug. 31, 2018; Andrew Perrin, "Stop Blaming Postmodernism for Post-Truth Politics," *Chronicle of Higher Education*, Aug. 4, 2017.

24. Asad Haider, "Critical Confusion," Aug. 1, 2020, https://asadhaider .substack.com/p/critical-confusion.

25. Quoted in Ruark, "Bait and Switch."

26. Quoted in Ruark, "Bait and Switch"; Hofstadter, *Anti-Intellectualism in American Life*, 21; Charlotte Lydia Riley, "Liz Truss doesn't know about Foucault, but she also doesn't care," *Guardian*, Dec. 19, 2020, deems postmodernism "one of those zombie ideas that cannot be killed by facts."

27. Quoted in Ruark, "Bait and Switch."

28. Christopher Newfield, "Academic Freedom as Democratization," *Academe*, 106, no. 2 (2020), 41-42.

29. Matthew C. Moen, "Opportunity Knocks for Liberal Education," *Inside Higher Ed*, Dec. 17, 2020.

30. Meranze, "For a Reparative University," 31.

31. "Academic Freedom and Tenure in the Quest for National Security: Report of a Special Committee of the American Association of University Professors," *AAUP Bulletin*, 42 (1956), 97.

Index

Abraham, David, 31-32
academic boycotts. *See* Boycott,
  Divestment, Sanctions (BDS)
  movement
academic capitalism, 41
academic freedom: academic
  boycotts and, 100; administrators and, 105-8; anti-
  intellectualism and, 185-87;
  artistic expression and, 51-53;
  balance and, 58-59; campus
  safety and, 96; classified
  research and, 36-40; conservative view of, 13-14; contingent
  faculty and, 24-25, 50-51, 74, 113,
  131-33; contract law and, 151-54;
  definition of, 2-4, 16-17;
  disciplinary standards and, 13;
  donors and, 45-49; expert
  knowledge and, 179-82; in
  extramural expression, 83-94;
  free speech and, 3, 8-9, 83-84,
  166; German source of, 6-7;
  hostile learning environment
  and, 60-66; indoctrination and,
  56-58; institutional, 138-43; in
  intramural expression, 110-14;
  IRBs and, 34-36; librarians and,
  23-24; limits on, 55, 61, 67, 70-71;
  in McCarthy era, 18, 135-38;
  open access and, 44-45; online

instruction and, 75-78; peer
  review and, 29-34; political
  activity and, 108-110; postmodernism and, 187-190; racial
  justice and, 18-20, 190-91; in
  religious institutions, 48-82; of
  students, 7, 20, 155-76; Supreme
  Court and, 134, 136-43, 160-62;
  tenure and, 116, 117, 119-20;
  unionism and, 23, 143-46,
  150-51. *See also* American
  Association of University
  Professors (AAUP); *Declaration
  of Principles on Academic Freedom
  and Academic Tenure* (1915);
  *Statement of Principles on
  Academic Freedom and Tenure*
  (1940); tenure
*Academic Freedom and Electronic
  Communications*, 76
*Academic Freedom and National
  Security in a Time of Crisis*, 38-39
*Academic Freedom and Tenure in the
  Quest for National Security*, 108,
  135-36, 207n4
academy-industry relationships,
  41-44
*Affirmative Action in Higher
  Education*, 19-20
Adelphi University, 57, 123
adjuncts. *See* contingent faculty

Adler, Patricia, 63
Alabama State College, 160
Alvin, Phil, 211n23
AMCHA Initiative, 101
American Academy of Arts and
  Sciences, 185
American Association of University
  Professors (AAUP): on academic
  boycotts, 100-101; on affirmative
  action, 19-20; amicus briefs by,
  42, 50, 64, 140; *Assignment of
  Course Grades and Student Appeals*,
  71-72; on classified research,
  38-39; Committee A, 17, 36, 56,
  62, 71, 89, 101; on common good,
  13; on Confucius Institutes,
  40-41; on contingent faculty,
  24-25; *Draft Statement on Student
  Participation in College and
  University Governance*, 167;
  *Enlargement of the Classified
  Information System*, 38; *Ensuring
  Academic Freedom in Politically
  Controversial Academic Personnel
  Decisions*, 119-20; on financial
  exigency, 122-23; formation of,
  9-10; *Freedom and Responsibility*,
  103; *Freedom in the Classroom*,
  56-58, 61, 67-69; Free Speech
  Movement (FSM) and, 158; on
  institutional review boards,
  35-36; investigations by, 14-15,
  24, 28, 51, 52, 57, 63-64, 67, 68,
  72-73, 79-80, 88-89, 90-91, 97,
  112, 114, 123-26, 135, 155, 171-72,
  218n16; on librarians, 23-24;
  *Mandated Assessment of Educa-
  tional Outcomes*, 74-75; Mississippi report (1963), 18-19; *National
  Security, the Assault on Science,
  and Academic Freedom*, 178; *On
  Academic Boycotts*, 100; *On the
  Relationship of Faculty Governance
  to Academic Freedom*, 111; on
  post-tenure review, 128-29; on
  recording of classroom statements, 77; response to 1950s
  anti-Communist scare, 4, 18, 90,
  108-9, 135, 192; *The Role of the
  Faculty in Conditions of Financial
  Exigency*, 122-23, 126; sexual
  harassment cases, 62-64; social
  media cases, 95-97; *Statement on
  Copyright*, 43, 45; *Statement on
  Extramural Utterances*, 89-90;
  Statement on Graduate Students,
  169-70; *Statement on Intellectual
  Property*, 78; *Statement on
  Professional Ethics*, 61; *Statement on
  Professors and Political Activity*,
  109; *Statement on Teaching
  Evaluation*, 73; on student rights
  and protests, 20, 61, 162-65,
  166-68, 173-74; on tenure, 17-18,
  24, 116-19; unionism and, 23,
  208n16; on university gover-
  nance, 20-22, 111; World War I
  patriotism and, 15. *See also*
  academic freedom; *Academic
  Freedom and Electronic Communi-
  cations*; *Academic Freedom and
  National Security in a Time of
  Crisis*; *Academic Freedom and
  Tenure in the Quest for National
  Security*; *Declaration of Principles
  on Academic Freedom and Academic
  Tenure* (1915); *In Defense of
  Knowledge and Higher Education*;
  *Joint Statement on the Rights and
  Freedoms of Students*; *Recom-
  mended Institutional Regulations on
  Academic Freedom and Tenure*;
  *Recommended Principles to Guide
  Academy-Industry Relationships*;
  *Statement of Principles on Academic
  Freedom and Tenure* (1940);

George Mason University, 46
George Washington University,
    105-6
Gersen, Jeannie Suk, 174
Gilman, Howard, 84, 157-58, 166,
    202
Gorman, Robert, 145
Gottschalk, Louis, 112
grading, 71-73
Greene v. Howard University,
    153

Hanlon, Aaron, 188
harassment, 1, 60-61, 94-95, 102,
    174, 178, 186. *See also* sexual
    harassment; social media
Harlan, Justice John, 137
Harvard University, 110
Heerden, Ivor van, 50-51
Hesburgh, Theodore, 79
Hofstadter, Richard, 81, 135, 185-87,
    189
Hook, Sidney, 108
Hoover Institution, 210n18
hostile learning environment,
    60-66
humanities, 41, 181-82, 185, 188,
    218n16

immigration, 39, 92
*In Defense of Knowledge and Higher
    Education*, 179-80, 183-84
indoctrination in teaching,
    56-58
in loco parentis, 55, 156-59,
    172-76
institutional governance. *See*
    shared governance
institutional review boards (IRBs),
    34-36
intellectual property, 39, 42-45, 78,
    170
intramural expression, 110-15

JASON, 40
*Joint Statement on Faculty Status of
    College and Research Librarians*,
    23-24
*Joint Statement on the Rights and
    Freedoms of Students*, 20, 61, 103,
    166-68

Kennedy, Justice Anthony, 148-49,
    150
Kirk, Russell, 13-14
Koch, Charles, 45-48. *See also*
    Charles Koch Foundation.
Koch, Leo, 88-90, 94, 214n7
Krislov, Samuel, 164-65
Kurland, Jordan, 120, 152-53

Lancet, 30
learning outcomes. *See* assessment
Lee, Philip, 152
lehrfreiheit, 7, 155-56
Lemann, Nicholas, 185
lernfreiheit, 7, 20, 155-56, 166, 176
letters of recommendation, 102-3
Levinson-Waldman, Rachel, 154
Lewy, Guenter, 165
Liberty University, 81-82
Limitations Clause. See *Statement
    of Principles on Academic Freedom
    and Tenure* (1940)
Louisiana State University, 50-51,
    63-64, 73
Lovejoy, Arthur, 83, 85-86, 112
Lukianoff, Greg, 175

Machlup, Fritz, 119-20, 127-28
Mann, Michael, 49
Marks, Jonathan, 175
Marquette University, 151-52
Marshall, Justice Thurgood, 140,
    143, 145
Marxism, 31, 57, 141
Mayer, Jane, 47